Sept. 1997

To Donnis,
    Best wishes Always
        Harambee!
            Grace Kuto.

Europe

Mediterranean Sea

Middle East

MOROCCO

TUNISIA

ALGERIA

LIBYA

EGYPT

WESTERN
SAHARA

MAURITANIA

MALI

NIGER

CHAD

SUDAN

DJIBOUTI

SENEGAL

THE GAMBIA

GUINEA
BISSAU

GUINEA

SIERRA
LEONE

LIBERIA

CÔTE
D'IVOIRE

BURKINA
FASO

BENIN

GHANA

TOGO

NIGERIA

CAMEROON

CENTRAL AFRICAN
REPUBLIC

ETHIOPIA

SOMALIA

EQUATORIAL
GUINEA

GABON

CONGO

ZAIRE

RWANDA

UGANDA

BURUNDI

KENYA

CABINDA
(ANGOLA)

TANZANIA

Indian
Ocean

Atlantic
Ocean

ANGOLA

ZAMBIA

MALAWI

ZIMBABWE

MOZAMBIQUE

MADAGASCAR

NAMIBIA

BOTSWANA

WALVIS BAY
(SOUTH AFRICA)

SWAZILAND

LESOTHO

SOUTH
AFRICA

0   500   1000 Miles

0   500   1000 Kilometers

Harambee!
African Family Circle
Cookbook

Grace Kuto

BookPartners, Inc.
Wilsonville, Oregon

BookPartners, Inc.
P. O. Box 922
Wilsonville, Oregon 97070

We all benefit from a greater and deeper understanding of each other's cultures. It is time to bring to our understanding of human life a greater sense of curiosity, acceptance and appreciation of those who are different. In choosing from your heart to respect the unique human spirit in all cultures, you are also choosing to expand your own potential.

The late Gladys McCoy
1928 - 1993

Dedication

This book is dedicated to my parents, Maria Muyoka Njunukha and Joel Wekhui Wasilwa and our extended family.

Portions of the proceeds from this book will go to the renovation of the four-wall Chwele Friends Dispensary/ Clinic to honor my parents' tireless and innovative services to their community through the Friends movement.

The dispensary is located on the campus of two elementary schools, Chwele Boys Primary School and Chwele Girls Primary School (1,200 students) and two high schools, Chwele Boys High School and Chwele Girls High School (1,400 students), and serves the student body as well as the community of about 15,000 people.

I treasure the memory of my parents.

Acknowledgements

First and foremost, I want to thank my husband, Paul, and our daughters, Muyoka and Lutomia for their diligent support of this writing. Often, they had to fend for themselves while I tended to activities related to this work. Through it all, we grew as a family. I especially want to thank our daughters for being a vital part of this book—it would not be the same without their contributions.

Mary Muyoka Kuto posed for the cover and Elizabeth Lutomia Kuto provided the food drawings.

My gratitude goes to my late parents to whom this book is dedicated. They introduced our family to the true value of hospitality. The seed they planted has grown. My brothers, sisters, uncles, aunts, brothers-in-law, sisters-in-law, nephews and nieces deserve a big "Thank You" for raising me with their endless care, love and support. From each and everyone of them, I learned something different but special. I feel blessed to have had so many fine role models in my life.

There are a great many people outside my family to whom I wish to express my gratitude:

Carolyn M. Leonard for writing the forward

Kenneth Howell of Portland, Oregon for the cover photography.

Allison Beach, one of my favorite high school teachers who supported my love for cooking.

Mary Khaemba Makokha for being my best friend through our school years and forever.

Howard and Bethlin Harmon of Newberg, Oregon for joining us in matrimony and supporting our relationship.

Dr. David Weil of Beaverton, Oregon, for seeing me through difficult pregnancies—both as a physician and as a friend.

Dr. Wage of Portland, Oregon, for caring for our premature daughters.

Nawanga Khalayi (Kathy Wilson) of Seattle, Washington, for supporting our family through a major illness and lovingly caring for Muyoka while I lived at the hospital.

Loretta Thorpe of Portland, Oregon for giving me the insight of "cooking for the heart."

Linda Hendrickson of Portland, Oregon for sharing her inspiration on African cooking with me. Linda visited and guided tours to Kenya in the 1980s. She single-handedly raised funds to build a permanent classroom— a harambee primary school near Nyeri, Kenya. Those unknown children who sit in that classroom know that some kind American lady did this for them. They are very grateful. Thank you Linda.

Kathryn Bogle of Portland, Oregon for her constant encouragement and support of this work.

Senator Bill McCoy of Portland, Oregon, for allowing me to use a quotation of his wife, the late honorable Gladys McCoy in this book.

Jill McDonald of Wilsonville, Oregon for allowing me to use her informative article on Kenya's climate.

Mary Lloyd for innovative ideas about the make up of

the book.

Dr. Alice Armstrong (my former professor) of Portland, Oregon for valuable advice.

Carolyn Leonard for contributing the foreword.

Onesmus Musundi for diligently helping with editing.

The Kenyan Women of Portland, Oregon and Seattle, Washington for their encouragement and support of this writing.

There are also several organizations which made this writing possible.

International Women's Day Festival (Portland Chapter).

Jane Hartline, marketing director of Washington Park Zoo.

American Heart Association.

Oregon Health Sciences University.

African Women Harambee Association.

Society of African Residents in North America.

World Affairs Council.

I owe my thanks to so many others who I am not able to mention here due to lack of space.

Asante Sana!

Grace Kuto

Foreword

In *Harambee! African Family Circle Cookbook,* Grace Kuto graciously shares the history and culture of East Africa and provides over 30 authentic recipes that reflect the cuisine of different ethnic groups of Kenya. She opens the world of East African culture.

In African tradition, Grace Kuto presents recipes which utilize ingredients and products readily available to rural people of her homeland. She offers selections that are low in fat and encourage the cook to make each step—the choice, the preparation and the blending of ingredients—an act that is carried out with love, happiness and in celebration of family and community.

The cookbook presents the reader with the opportunity to prepare a complete and authentic East African meal or simply select one item to be included with other dishes.

Harambee! demonstrates easy-to-follow recipes. In the spirit of African tradition, you can share these delicious ethnic dishes, and at the same time learn about African culture, including the meaning and importance of families working together to build a stronger community.

Harambee! Let's Pull Together!

Carolyn M. Leonard
Coordinator of Multicultural and Multi-Ethnic Education
Portland Public Schools

Table Of Contents

Introduction

Harambee! (pronounced har-ahm-bay) means "lets pull together" in the spirit of giving. It is a Swahili (Kenya's national language) word that symbolizes the idea that people working together make a significant difference in a community than one person working alone.

The *Harambee! African Family Circle Cookbook* was born and written in this very spirit. Traditional African families gather in a circle at meal time and eat together. The circle exemplifies the spirit of sharing and togetherness.

I collected the recipes in this book from family members and friends. I developed some of them by accident, others were born from curiosity. I have shared these delicious dishes in Portland with thousands of people at numerous multi-cultural community and school events, as well as at our home for more than 15 years.

I now want to bring these easy and delicious recipes to people beyond the borders of Portland and Kenya. In Africa, the assembling and sharing of food highlights the spirit of celebration and the daily bonding of family and the community. The recipes offer a look at the basics of the African cultural eating habits and values. Traditional African cooking is most adventurous, yet least known in the international cooking arena.

The African continent is vast and is the home for many different people, and it is difficult to characterize some "African dishes" as "typically African." The more contemporary East African cooking is influenced by East Asian and European tastes because of the political history these cultures have shared with this particular African region.

This book mainly concentrates on the traditional cooking of East Africa. In African urban areas herbs and spices are more commonly used. In rural areas, traditional habits of cooking and eating have almost remained unchanged by outside influences. The traditional African customs encompass not just the satisfaction of hunger but are strong means for enhancing family and community ties.

People eating together in the African community is one of the most meaningful aspects of the culture. One rarely eats alone. Food is also used an expression of celebration at weddings, babies' birthdays or naming ceremonies, community harambee gatherings, family reunions, funerals, welcoming guests and so on. A first-time guest is always acknowledged with a feast of a meal. In times of scarcity, not much may be available to share, but the little still must be divided among those in the circle. Western observers are often amazed at the mountains of food which are prepared for typical African weddings. The leftovers are happily shared and bags of food leave the party along with the happy guests.

This book also addresses how traditional African food and lifestyles affect the health of the people. Eaten in right amounts and combinations, the East African diet is ideal for maintaining good health. An average rural African family eats more plant foods than animal foods simply because they are readily available. Meat is not eaten more than two or three times a week—especially in rural areas. Studies point to the long-term health effects the East African diet and the lifestyle have on its people.

A study conducted by cardiologist, M. John Murray, of the University of Minnesota, looks at the specific components of the Masai diet and how it is affected by their lifestyle.

Another recent study conducted by Kenyan medical experts disclosed that incidences of hypertension among the Masai and Samburu tribes are almost non-existent. It proves that those ethnic groups who have maintained traditional lifestyles and diets have managed to escape the dilemma of food and industry-related diseases such as heart attacks, strokes, diabetes, certain cancers and other serious health problems. This book emphasizes the importance of a well balanced diet, rich in nutritional values. Basic nutrition facts are discussed so that the reader has a basic understanding of food and the chemical interactions which take place in the human body.

In Africa, food and hospitality are synonymous with the African woman. A section of this book is dedicated to her contribution to food productivity in her homeland.

I wrote the poem "The Heart of Africa" in memory of

my mother, and for all the African women whose strength holds the cultural fabric of their society together.

I have dedicated the poem "The Hungry Child of Africa," to the needy children of my homeland.

Mini Facts On Kenya

Official name:	Republic of Kenya.
Location:	East Africa (see map of Africa).
Area:	224,960 square miles (580,367 square kilometers).
Population:	26 million (1992 estimate).
Ethnic groups:	40 or more ethnic groups using different languages or dialects. The main ones are: African; Kikuyu 21%, Luhya 14%, Luo 13%, Kalenjin 11%, Kamba 11%, Kisii 6%, Meru 5%. Non-African; Asian, European, Arab combined 1%.
Religions:	Indigenous beliefs 24%, Protestant 40%,

	Roman Catholic 30%, Muslim 6%.
Languages:	Swahili (national language), English and many ethnic local languages.
Greeting:	Strong, firm handshake and eye contact whether male or female.
Education:	First four years of primary school are free; eight years primary, four years high school and four years college or university.
Work Force:	Total wage earners 1.4 million: public sector 48%, industry and commerce 21%, agriculture 21%.
Colonial History:	Kenya's written history dates back to 1,000 BC. Kenya's proximity to the Arabian Peninsula invited colonization. Arab and Persian settlers were the first in the area about the eighth century. By then the Bantu and Nilostic peoples had already moved into the area. The Kiswahili language, a mixture of Arabic, English and other languages became the trading language. In 1498, Portuguese arrived and took over from the Arabs at the coast. About 1600, the Imam of Oman reigned until the British laid claim to the whole of East Africa and declared the land mass a protectorate in 1895. Kenya officially became a British colony in 1920. From October 1952 to December 1959, Kenya was under a state emergency which arose from Mau Mau (Muzungu Aende Ulaya, Muafrica Apate

Uhuru) revolution against the British colonial rule. During the colonial time, there was segregation in Kenya just like it was in the United States and South Africa. The first direct elections for Africans to the Legislature Council took place in 1957. Kenya became independent in 1963 and joined the Commonwealth the following year. Jomo Kenyatta, a member of the Kikuya tribe and head of the Kenya African National Union (KANU) became Kenya's first president. When President Kenyatta died in August 1978, Vice President Daniel Arap Moi became the interim president and in October 1978 was elected the second president of Kenya and is still in power at this writing.

Main Sources
of Foreign
Exchange: Coffee, tea and pyrethrum exports, tourism and petroleum products.

Monetary unit: Kenyan shilling.

Kenya Embassy: Address: Embassy of Kenya, 2249 R. Street N. W., Washington, DC 20008 - Telephone: 202-387-6101

Kenya Consulate: Telephone: 310-274-6635

The Climate Of Kenya

The Climate Of Kenya: Its Effect On The Culture was written by Jill McDonald, born and raised in Kenya, resident of Wilsonville, Oregon

It has been said that Kenya has the best climate in the world — and for part of the country this could certainly be true.

Climate, anywhere in the world, influences the types of foods people eat, their occupations, modes of transport, their homes, dress and all other facets of life. In fact, weather influences their culture.

In Kenya, because the land varies in altitude from sea level to heights over 17,000 feet, there are areas of desert, tropical forest, dry grassland, alpine meadows, equatorial lowlands, and rich farmland. Each of these regions calls for its inhabitants to make adaptations in lifestyle and so encourages cultural differences between the various tribes. The vast majority of Kenyans live at altitudes of 3,000 to 6,000 feet above sea level.

As a result of Kenya spanning the Equator, the country experiences no real winter. Only the wetter periods of the monsoon convey the feeling of having seasons. Regions less affected by rains are the vast deserts or semi-deserts in the north, east and south of the country.

Due to being located in the proximity of the Equator, every day of the year has the same amount of daylight—there is no switch from "Daylight Saving Time" to Standard Time. There is no sunset at five o'clock one day and at nine o'clock another day. A constant twelve hours of night and twelve hours of day is the rule. The sun rises at around 6:30 a.m. and sets at around 6:30 p.m. every day of the year.

In the highland regions of Kenya there is sufficient rainfall, as well as excellent soil. Food staples such as corn, rice, potatoes, vegetables and fruits can be grown. The natives have a balanced diet. In the lower more arid areas this is not the case. Many tribes rely more on the meat products from their cattle and goats—no spinach is grown there. Along the coastal strip, where the climate is more tropical, fish and coconuts feature prominently in the diet.

Even the dress of Kenyans is influenced by the climate. Throughout most of the country the people like to wear strong bright colors: reds, yellows, blues, greens, pinks and oranges. These hues match the bright sunshine. Some exceptions to this are the Maasai, Turkana and Samburu people who live a nomadic life. They wander over the hot, dusty plains with their herds of cattle and goats.

They have largely retained their preference for using earthy tones in their garments — especially the reddish brown blankets in which they wrap themselves. Another exception is the women from the northeastern and eastern regions who, because of their Moslem faith wear black robes. The men of the coastal region are often seen in white clothing, which reflects the extreme heat.

The types of homes in which Kenyans live are affected by climate and location. As a result of the arid climate which dictates a nomadic lifestyle, the Maasai, Turkana, Samburu and other pastoral tribes had to be able to literally "pick up stick" and move their houses frequently in order to gain access to fresh grazing land for their herds. They have largely built easily moveable homes which can quickly be reassembled. Traditionally, the homes of farming peoples from the higher, fertile, more temperate regions have been constructed for permanence from the products of the forests and grasslands that surround them. In this region, the nights can be quite cold so the need for warmth and a good chimney hole is important. The rondavaal, made of mud and wattle, was the traditional home of Kikuyu and other tribes. More recently these have been replaced with larger, even longer-lasting, wooden and stone structures. The residents of the hot coastal lowlands need their shelter more from the heat than from the cold. They have cut the poles for their homes from the nearby mangrove swamps and roofed them with palm fronds.

People from the agricultural highland, which has a climate that allows for the constant renewal of crops, have not been faced with the need to make frequent moves to greener pastures. They have been able to become expert farmers, and industrious business people and government employees. The nomadic people remain largely as wanderers since they must cater to their herds' constant needs. The coastal Kenyans have, until recently, concentrated on occupations related to fishing and trading with foreign nations at their ports.

Kenya's excellent climate is a major attraction, along with the wildlife, which brings thousands of tourists each year and with it foreign currency for the country's economy.

The Kiswahili Language In East Africa

Kiswahili is the recognized national language in Kenya and Tanzania since the two countries became independent. It is also widely spoken in Uganda and Zaire, and more recently has spread into other central and southern countries such as Angola, Zambia, Zimbabwe and Mozambique. It is the mother tongue of a group of people along the East African coast and the islands inhabited by the Swahili people. These people descended from members of many nations who came to trade along the East African coast as early as 1600 A.D. — Arabs, Portuguese, Persians and Europeans. Kiswahili is a combination of several languages, including English, and is very easy to learn.

In Kenya and Tanzania, Kiswahili is used in broadcasting, publications—books, magazines, journals, newspapers and written correspondence. It is spoken in official public addresses and used in some curriculum at lower grades.

Kiswahili is not generally spoken in tribal homes in rural areas. In urban areas however, more and more Kiswahili is used by those who come from different tribes. The average Kenyan speaks his or her vernacular in the home, uses Kiswahili in market places or when interacting with a different tribal member. English is spoken in schools and office settings.

As for tribal languages, there are over 40 ethnic groups in Kenya alone who all speak different dialects. It is quite common for Kenyans to speak more than a few different dialects in addition to Kiswahili and English. Since different languages are nothing out of the ordinary in the East African culture, introducing foreign languages is encouraged in schools, because East Africa is involved in foreign trade with countries all over the world. The most commonly studied foreign languages in Kenyan schools are French, German and Italian. English and Kiswahili are required language subjects in high schools in Kenya.

Swahili Words ... a visitor to East Africa will find useful when trying to communicate in Kiswahili.

Here's How The Vowels Sound:

a	as in man
e	as in men
i	as in pin
o	as in hope
u	as in Uganda

Bicycle	Barsikeli
Brother	Kaka
Bus	Basi
Car	Gari
Come	Njoo
Church	Kanisa
Father	Baba
Food	Chakula
Freedom	Uhuru
Hello	Jambo
Here	Hapa
How are you?	Habari
I want	Nataka
I don't want	Sitaki
Let's pull together	Harambee
Me	Mimi
Money	Pesa
Mother	Mama
No	Hapana

Please	Tafaahali (Tafathali)
Road	Barabara
Shilling	Shilingi
Sister	Dada
Thank you	Asante
Taxi	Taksi
Time	Saa
Toilet	Choo
Us	Sisi
Very much	Sana
Water	Maji
Well	Mzuri
What is the time?	Saa ngapi
Where	Wapi
Who	Nani
Yes	Ndio
You	Wewe
You (plural)	Nyinyi

To learn more Swahili :
Teach Yourself Swahilii - by D.V. Perrott
Hodder & Stoughton, Ltd. Great Britain.

What's in a Name?

Semantic Differences

American	British
Excuse me	I am sorry
Elevator	Lift
Two weeks	Fortnight
Ride	Lift
Recess	Break
Pressing	Ironing
Apartment	Flat
Call	Ring
Diaper	Napkin
Napkin	Serviette
Baby Buggy	Pram
Guy	Chap
Bracelet	Bangle
Get off	Alight
Purse	Handbag
Wallet	Purse
Peanuts	Groundnuts
Cookies	Bisquits
Candy	Sweets
Toilet	Water Closet
Resume	Vitae
Football	Soccer
Tuition	Fees
Grade	Class
Grade School	Primary School
High School	Secondary School

Diploma	Degree
Raisins	Currants
Glasses	Spectacles
Gasoline	Petrol
Rubbing Alcohol	Spirit
Bandaid	Elastoplast
Dinner	Supper
Hamburger Meat	Minced Meat
Basketball	Net Ball
Patio	Veranda
Pill	Tablet
Full	Satisfied

How To Use This Book

African people rarely consult recipes for their meal preparations. Cooking is an art —cooking without measurements—mostly acclaimed by women. In my tribe, a newly-married woman who does not demonstrate cooking skills— especially for the staple foods like Ugali — may be sent back to her family for additional training. No family ever wants their daughter to be returned to them for lack of simple cooking skills. The bride's family members always make sure that the young woman is a good cook before she gets married. There are no written recipes included in the list of ceremonial marriage gifts.

This book is written to encourage readers to experiment with African foods in their home. I hope the recipes will evoke the reader's own culinary creativity.

First try the original recipe then create your very own "African" dish by omitting or adding certain ingredients when appropriate. Recipes in this book can be prepared for:

- potlucks.
- multi-cultural exchange celebrations.
- wedding celebrations.
- birthday celebrations.
- anniversary celebrations.
- ethnic and multi-cultural curricula in schools.
- a healthy hearty African meal.

Certain methods of cooking have been modified to promote healthier food habits: instead of boiling vegetables, steaming is recommended when possible.

The recipes which meet the American Heart Association guidelines are marked with ♥

Most of the ingredients can be found in regular grocery stores if you live in a fairly large city in the United States. Some of the ingredients may only be available in specialty stores which cater to African, Caribbean, Indian, Spanish or Oriental clientele. In Canada and England most of the ingredients may be available in specialty stores only. In Kenya, all the ingredients are sold in open markets. Some of you — your friends or relatives — may even grow some of the plants in your gardens.

Benefits Of This Book

1. A portion of the proceeds of this book will go to support several African projects and causes in American and African communities. These projects and causes may be chosen by you, by your churches, schools, private agencies, or by the author herself. (See next page for more information on how you, your church, school or private agency can utilize this book to support your African projects.)

This book ...

- Serves as an intercultural information reference resource to African-American communities all over the United States.
- Is an additional resource on African culture to the

existing but limited information in ethnic school curricula throughout America.

- Serves as an important source of information to the young, lay and student populations throughout Africa, as well as preserving African tradition for future generations. Some Africans are no longer experiencing the same family support outlined in this book due to the changing family structure in Africa caused by urbanization and other elements of change. Africa is mainly an oral society. For centuries, traditions and customs were handed down from generation to generation by mouth. Times are changing and like other parts of the world, Africa is fast losing its traditions.
- Provides basic nutrition information encouraging the reader to develop healthy eating habits.
- Invites the reader to experiment with different foods from other parts of the world. Food has always been a common denominator in global relationships. Learning about the different "tastes" of another culture more than likely heightens the interest to know more about that country through travel, reading or interacting with people from that culture.
- Exposes the reader to palatable dishes through the use of herbs and spices.

African Women and Food

The subject of food in Africa is synonymous with the role of women in that culture.

Although the vital contribution to food production by women in Africa is routinely overlooked, the awareness of their role in countries with poor economies has increased since the beginning of the United Nations Decade for Women in 1975. This issue was addressed with more emphasis when the Second World Women Conference was held in Nairobi, Kenya in 1985, and will be taken up again in 1995 at the Third Decade Conference in Beijing, China.

In Africa alone, women account for 80 percent of the agricultural labor force according to United Nations statistics. In situations where men have moved to the cities in search of work, rural women have been left without help for carrying water, fetching firewood, clearing land, sowing, weeding and harvesting crops. On top of growing the food for meals and preparing them, women rear their children and attend to the chores in their homes.

Throughout the colonial period (from early 1900s to late 1950s), African women were denied formal education. In more recent times, developmental aid projects have been initiated by women's self-help groups (harambee groups) as well as the government to help meet family needs for clean and accessible water, replenishable sources of fuel and energy-saving devices such as improved cooking stoves.

Despite the heavy burden on the African woman, she is blessed with a boundless spirit of hospitality that is cherished in the community and throughout the African society. She is the thread that holds the African cultural fabric together. Family bonding and support enable her the strength to carry on, even at the worst of times.

The visitor who is fortunate enough to experience the African family circle and share what people offer so generously—no matter how desperate the circumstances—will have gained an enduring lesson in giving the most precious gift of all, the gift of self.

When the African woman prepares food, she always cooks more than her family requires, because neighbors, friends, extended family or even a stranger are likely to drop in during meal time. If you find an African family eating together, you are expected to join in the celebration of sharing.

I enjoy sharing African foods and recipes with my friends and neighbors. I hope that you use this book and these recipes in the spirit of the discovery of new foods and giving of self.

Cooking Methods In East Africa

Refrigeration is not available in rural areas in East Africa. Meals are prepared daily, fresh from the garden or purchased at the open market. Most of the rural families still use the three-stone cooking method to prepare their meals.

Three medium-size stones are placed in a hollow in the ground, forming a circle. Firewood is piled in the center and lit. The cooking temperature is controlled by the amount of wood added to the crackling fire. The *sufuria* (deep sauce pan) is settled firmly on top of the three stones over the flames. The smell of the wood fire and the aroma of the simmering food permeate the air with tantalizing results.

When the British came to East Africa they introduced

wood stoves with ovens, which were followed by gas and electric stoves in the urban areas. During that time kerosene and paraffin contraptions were being used, and the invention of the *jiko*— a brazier— became a popular cooking convenience. The *jiko* is fueled by charcoal made from wood and is still being used for cooking in both urban and rural areas.

In many ways, life is still quite simple and uncomplicated by buttons and dials of sophisticated equipment in East Africa, which seems to fit the character of the small communities quite well.

In my own automated kitchen in Portland, I appreciate the convenience of pushing buttons, getting instant heat to cook our meals, heat the house, cool jugs of milk, wash our clothes and be "climate-controlled." But at times it seems artificial and sterile.

I miss getting down on my knees to tend the dying fire that glimmers between the smooth surface of the time-tested cooking stones. I miss the pungent smell of the rich, dark earth, and the roasting of green maize during the evening, in the warm presence, the chatter and the laughter of my family.

I remember how my brothers and sister taught me to count with the help of the grains of maize as we ate them. It was a delightful way of learning for me, because it was associated with "eating."

Most of all, as a woman now, I miss the camaraderie, the story-telling, the laughter, the tears, the exchange of ideas and the benign gossip that took place in the Kenya kitchen of my youth. Now, I teach my daughters how to cook with me, and we use that time to talk about school, friends, activities, growing pains and family matters. I love to cook with them.

Family Background

My love and appreciation for cooking stemmed from the influence my own childhood family exerted. I come from a large family of twelve siblings (six girls and six boys) of whom I am the youngest. Three brothers and one sister are deceased. In the African culture, the youngest child holds a special place in the family, and is the recipient of a lot of affection from everybody in the clan. Superstition or not, it is sometimes believed that the youngest child has certain special powers. In my sub-tribe, the youngest child is known (not incorrectly) as *Mutua,* meaning the "womb locker." All my brothers and sisters call me by *Mutua* instead of Grace.

Grace is my Christian name. My African name is *Nasiebanda* which means survivor because I was overdue at birth. My mother encountered severe health problems at the end of her pregnancy and it was uncertain whether she and I would survive. When we both did, my mother told my oldest sister that we were alive only by the "grace" of God. The two women decided to name me Grace. My name carries a lot of meaning for me and that is why I still use it. I love my African name too because I have survived so many ordeals in life. I am a survivor!

Home was a large, multi-room, thatched farmhouse in the village of Chwele. After my parents died I went to live with another sister and her husband in a roomy, modern permanent house in the village of Chesikaki. That big house has been donated to the community and now serves as a reconciliation center and clinic. During my high school years, I lived in Nairobi, but always returned home for the school holidays.

Since I am the youngest, I saw only one of my four grandparents. My maternal grandfather known as Njunukha was still alive. He had fought in the First World War for the British against the Germans, and was over 100 years old when he died in the early sixties. My mother was his *Mutua* and he loved her immensely. For years he told us stories from the big war and the part of the world we had not seen. There was a deep bond and love between us.

My parents, Joel Wekhui Wasilwa and Maria Muyoka Njunukha died in their mid-fifties when I was about eight-years old. My father was born about 1898 and died in 1956. Six years later, my mother, who was born in 1908, passed away. My parents were among the first generation of Africans to become Friends (Quakers) — who, by the way, were the first to speak out and act against slavery in

America.

My mother and father were always actively engaged in community affairs, and through Friends learned about the values of a western education. They learned how to read and write, were looked upon as leaders, and mentored not just their own offspring but all the children in the community in the important values of becoming concerned and responsible adults.

Joel Wasilwa was a many gifted and innovative man. He was a tailor, a carpenter, farmer, teacher and soccer coach. (Two of his students married my two oldest sisters). He was a popular coach because he taught traditional values and ethics along with soccer rules. He had to do a lot of things in order to be able to send his children to school. He owned a maize grinding machine, an ox cart and plough and established a co-operative organization for selling cash crops. He was tireless in his efforts encouraging his clanspeople to send their children to school. In 1952 my oldest sister became the first trained and qualified, female teacher in our village.

My mother was a remarkable person as well. She was one of the best farmers in our area. She had a golden touch with everything that grew in the earth, she raised the best vegetables and the most flavorful herbs. On the land around our home, we grew lemons, oranges, *grandilia* (passion fruit), guavas, coffee, maize (corn), beans, millet, sorghum, sesame seeds, groundnuts (peanuts), cassava (yucca), sweet potatoes, pumpkins, Irish potatoes, bananas, squash, cabbage, kale, *sukuma wiki* (collard greens), onions, cowpeas leaves and several other varieties of African wild vegetables all year round. My father also kept a bee hive in our homestead and everyone enjoyed the fragrant, golden, sweet taste of honey.

Mother was an exceptionally gifted cook and house-wife, and an exemplary mother to her own children as well as a mentor to countless children of the community. There was always plenty of food in the house and she saw to it that no one in the circle ever went hungry.

Since my mother lived longer than my father, I developed a special bond with her. She sang to me every day and carried me on her back almost all the time until I was about five years old and had grown too big and heavy for her.

She had a highly developed gift for counseling, the ability to settle squabbles, spent endless hours helping people reconcile their differences, and made the act of forgiveness a virtue. She passed on her qualities to everyone she raised and mentored. My parents were the light of my life, and I only wish I could have had them longer.

I was raised by my oldest sister and my brother-in-law, Nora and John Musundi, who sacrificed many of their needs for the sake of my welfare. They sent me to the best schools they could afford, and gave me a structured set of values for life. My other older brothers, sisters and their spouses helped raise the rest of us too.

Taking care of the young ones by the older siblings is a common practice in Africa which again is the result of the strong family ties, a set of indisputable values and a sense for tradition—all of which are faithfully practiced in daily living. Even though I was quite young at the time of my parents death, I had already learned the value of hospitality from them, and later on, from the rest of my large family.

My parents welcomed, fed and hosted extended family members, friends, students and strangers in our home daily. My mother was known near and far for her "Mother Theresa" virtues. The door to our home was always open and preparing food was one part of welcoming and caring for visitors as well as the family.

I had so many fine teachers in my life, and I am grateful to all of them. My sisters, sisters-in-law and one particular niece, Nekoye, who grew up in our home reinforced my understanding of the value of African hospitality. I observed our customs and had hands-on instructions for the preparation of food under their dedicated guidance. They taught me the innovative art of African cooking.

I learned to cook with a "pinch"of this, a "touch" of that and a "bit and a splash" of this and that. I learned to judge the consistency of a stew by stirring it, and trained my sense of smell to tell me when things were "just" right.

My brothers taught me to appreciate nature, and from my three younger brothers I learned how different foods grow. They taught me the art of cultivating the land, and caring for the plants by hand with an African hoe.They showed me how to hunt birds in the wild with a *fandiri* (sling,) and how to trap birds right outside our kitchen. When I tagged along with my brothers while they tended the small herd of the family cattle, I picked up the names of birds, insects, plants and wild animals.

My favorite winged friends were, and still are, those beautiful, exotic butterflies. I have always been fascinated by their brilliant hues and intricate designs. I loved to watch them flutter from flower to wild flower in a dance of swirling colors enhanced by the bright sunlight against a blue African sky. As a child, I saw my mother's heart in the splendor of a butterfly. I knew that she had the most beautiful heart on earth—the heart that gave out of love for everyone who was fortunate enough to know her. She was a woman of very few words but she could move mountains with her quiet acts of faith. I find myself as bound to her these many years later, as I was as a child.

One of my brothers raised and tamed more than 20 doves which lived in my mother's kitchen. At home, the kitchen was in a separate hut a bit removed from the house, and one of my favorite places. The doves drove my mother nuts whenever she was cooking. I did not understand why she had so much patience with my brother. Now that I am a mother, I think I understand.

During the many hours I spent in the wild with my brothers, I smelled the fragrance of the beautiful flowers, touched wiggly insects, listened to the singing birds, the noises of big animals, and the burbling sounds of the clean streams flowing through the land.

In awe, I witnessed the brilliantly blending colors of rainbows arching high above the earth after a warm drizzly rain and felt the cool breezes rushing down from the very top of Mt. Elgon and brush against my face. I learned to appreciate the magnificence of nature. Well, not everything, I never did like all those slithery, crawly snakes.

We spent a lot of time outdoors on the land, and ate our fill from many Vitamin C-rich varieties of African wild fruits and berries. I liked being with my brothers and enjoyed that kind of life, especially since I didn't have their responsibility of watching the cattle. Our livestock was not only a source of food, but helped plough the land, and were traditional wedding gifts to family members starting out on their own.

I began grade school during the colonial period. During that era there were hardly any proper schools for African children in Kenya, other than a few missionary schools. At my first grade school, Kimabole, we had no classrooms for first and second graders. We had no books, pencils or note papers. Our classrooms were under the sweeping branches of tall trees. We wrote in the dirt with our index finger to demonstrate to our teachers what we had learned. In advancing grades, we used black slates and white chalk to practice our penmanship. Each student had one slate for all the subjects.

Because of my parents' commitment to education, I was exposed to a great deal of additional learning at home. By the time I was in sixth grade, three of my sisters had become trained teachers. One of my brothers, Javan (deceased) was particularly insistent on teaching me how to use the dictionary.

One evening, while helping me with my homework, he asked me to bring him "Michael West." I went to his bedroom to look for that person. I looked everywhere, even under the bed. I returned to my brother and told him that I couldn't find "Michael West."

Javan worked the issue a little longer, poking fun at me. He finally told me that the missing person was one of the authors of an English dictionary he owned. I trudged back to his room, located the big reference book and brought him his "Michael West." I enjoyed the the way he introduced me to the dictionary, and have valued its contents ever since.

When Kenya became independent in 1963, President Jomo Kenyatta's priority for developing the country was to build more schools, and many of them were built by parents through the harambee projects. In Kenya, I also attended Chwele Girls' Primary School, Lugulu Girls' Boarding School, and Alliance Girls' High School. Later I attended Chiswick Polytechnic in West London, England for two years. Finally, I attended Portland State University where I completed majors in business administration and business education (undergraduate and graduate levels respectively).

While at Portland State University, Paul and I got married. We had two "miracle" daughters. Muyoka (Mary) named after my mother and Lutomia (Elizabeth) named after Paul's aunt. Muyoka weighted two pounds at birth and Lutomia even less — she weighed all of one pound and a half. Both young girls have visited Kenya twice and have the fondest memories of our families and the closeness of the family circle.

I am grateful for the wealth of my African heritage, my beloved parents, my early school days and the blending of a western education, life on three continents, with the values, tradition and the beauty of my homeland.

If I have learned anything — it is *Harambee!* — the *pulling together* of a few for the benefit of all

The African Family Circle

In most of the world communities, the value of the family institution is recognized as the very foundation of civilizations. In Africa, family life is especially important to everyone because of the combined strength and support it holds for the individual.

In the Western culture, the term family refers to members of the immediate family. In the African culture family means grandparents, parents and children, uncles, aunts, cousins, brothers-in-law, sisters-in-law—the extended family. Each extended family is the major component of a clan. A clan stems from a sub-tribe which in turn is a part of a tribe (see chart below). There are about 40 sub-tribes in

Kenya.

My family tribe	=	Luhya.
My sub-tribe	=	Bukusu.
My maiden clan	=	Bakhoma.
My married clan	=	Bakokho.

Each clan is considered to share the same blood lines. Marrying within the same clan limits access to a genetic variety which leads to a high degree of vulnerability of passing on hereditary diseases.

That is why it is critical for young dating couples to identify each other's clans before the relationship starts. Typical African parents from certain tribes (the first time a couple meets) upon meeting the "intended" immediately ask to what clan he or she belongs

If one or the other is closely related to his or her respective clan by blood, the continuation of the courtship is generally discouraged.

Clan members usually relate to each other as if they come from the same nuclear family. Many of the sub-tribes use relationship titles to address family members in order to maintain mutual respect, especially for older family members.

Following is an example of my own sub-tribe:

Paternal uncle	=	father (papa).
Maternal uncle	=	uncle (khocha).
Paternal aunt	=	aunt (senge).
Maternal aunt	=	mother (mayi/mama).
Male cousin/brother	=	brother (wandase).
Female cousin/sister	=	sister (yaya).

These relationships contribute to the deep feelings of identifying with a family, and manifest in a strong sense of belonging. Belonging gives one a feeling of worth and honor, of being somebody and of being recognized as a welcome member in the midst of caring and loving people.

Children especially need the security of that all encompassing circle of recognition, appreciation and affection. Those youngsters who go without that emotional shelter are looking for it in all the wrong places. They find it in the back alleys of humanity. Gangs and dangerous cliques become the substitute family, and, unlike a real family, those alliances most often end in tragedy. This is happening all over the world as the family structure of the past disintegrates and many of the world's children threaten to become the rubble of the future.

In my own clan, the demonstration of the traditional cultural respect is in the way in-laws of the opposite sex greet each other. They do not shake hands or hug when they meet, and keep a certain physical distance between themselves as they honor each other's presence.

Each relative is viewed as having a specific value in terms of his or her role in relationship to the rest of the family members, and is looked upon as an individual with special gifts. Though each family member is respected as an individual, he or she is even more appreciated as being a part of the whole family team.

Extended African families are inter-dependent socially, emotionally and economically, and the children in the clan are disciplined, guided and loved by all the members. The children have the freedom to express their needs and concerns to any one family member with whom they feel most comfortable.

Sometimes, when parental patience runs out for a while, children can always turn to relatives for a breather who are only too glad to help out. Hence the saying "It takes a whole village to raise a child."

The vast majority of Africans do not have a Social Security income, welfare subsidies, life insurance policies or pensions. According to the Kenya government statistics (1992) only a small percentage of 26 million people are wage earners. Therefore the chain of responsibility is passed on to the next generation.

When someone depends on an older brother, sister or uncle for handling school tuition, the benefactor does not expect to have his money paid back. However, tradition requires the recipient to extend that same sharing to the younger members in the family who in turn will do the same.

You may ask just what the extended family circle has to do with African cooking?

It has everything to do with it.

The cycle of sharing begins when most African families gather in a circle to eat their meals.

Generally, the women prepare the food together. During that time they tell their stories, discuss events, and give advice to each other. Meeting and working together in itself is a strong bonding process. Since African families are generally large, children are usually served their meals in a separate circle. In rural Africa today, the majority of families still eat in a circle, helping themselves to their portion from one big bowl or dish which has been placed in the center of the circle.

The tradition of the circle automatically trains children at a very young age to share with other family members. A child typically wants to eat until his hunger is satisfied. When there isn't enough food to go around, the children eventually learn to look out for each other. Learning to share food in the family circle affects the children's behavior in all the other aspects of their lives. They are able to look out for each other while playing, fighting, working, studying, etc. The adult family members set the example for sharing at meal time.

Traditionally, Africans do not drink alcohol to get drunk, but consider the gathering to join in a drink a purely friendly, social occasion. At an African drinking party, the villagers sit in a circle and sip from long straws dipped into a big pot containing the customary brew. Between slow sips, they discuss life in general and philosophize about the aspects of living and dying. The elders lend their wisdom to the circle and teach their views on marriage, child rearing, and ethics to the younger people. If a person gets drunk, he is asked to leave the circle and is escorted home.

It's almost inevitable that during meal time a visitor drops in. Whatever food is left is shared with the drop-in. If the visitor turns down the offer to eat, then his motive for the visit is questioned by the family, and the moment can become quite uncomfortable. But customs in Africa are quite delicate, and when visitors are given the choice whether or not to eat, the gesture is not considered an invitation and the guests' declining is acceptable. In the event of a visitor bearing news of a family loss, his declining to eat is accepted.

If the guest has a good reason for not eating and the family accepts the excuse as solid, she gets to take home a live chicken in place of the meal she would have shared otherwise.

Eating together is a genuine gesture of acknowledging one another. Meals can last for several hours, and during that time the family reinforces the sense of caring and sharing—which in turn strengthens the family structure, fosters kinship and a sense of belonging which then carries over into the community.

The act of sharing becomes as natural as breathing for everyone. I remember when I was about eight years old, one of my sisters gave me my very own new pair of shoes. True to the spirit in which I was raised, I immediately gave one shoe to my best friend who was my age and with whom I shared just about everything. My family was not aware of my generous act. One day after a heavy rain fall, one of my sisters asked me to put on my shoes and accompany her on an errand. I showed up at her side, ready to leave, wearing my one shoe.

She asked where my other shoe was, and with child-like innocence, I told he that I had given it to my best friend, Nanjala. I could tell she was upset but instead of getting angry, she had to laugh. She then explained to me that sharing was a fine thing to do, but there were certain things one can't share. Shoes must be worn in a pair — one shoe really doesn't do anyone any good. I did get my shoe back, but whenever my friend needed shoes, I gladly lent her mine.

At times when there isn't enough food to go around, the positive emotional interaction that takes place in the family circle during a meal makes up for the void. Food is a feast for the body as well as for the spirit. That is one of the several reasons, I believe, why so many Africans are not overweight. People rarely eat alone.

Meal time is synonymous with family togetherness. When settling down to eat in the circle, people are rarely in a hurry, because eating takes place when most of the work for the day is done. The family members are relaxed and at ease with each other. They appreciate the offerings of the table and enjoy their meal in a leisurely fashion. Nobody has his eye on the clock. Their level of relaxation is at a high which aids the natural process of digesting food because the body produces the right proportion of digestive enzymes.

A time-honored tradition that makes this family time special is the hand-washing process before every meal. Family members pour water over each other's hands and wash them with soap in a basin or large bowl. This custom creates an atmosphere of respect and honor between the two people involved in the simple ceremony. It is especially heart-warming and therapeutic for the person receiving the water. To gently pour water over someone else's hands says "I care about you."

The next time you wash up before a meal, have a family member or friend pour water over your hands while you wash. See how it feels!

The bonding of the African family continues to grow as some family members get older. The elderly and the very young are especially close to each other and are the most valued members of society. The elderly always live in their homes with members of their extended family.

The oldest son usually doesn't moves away from his father's compound. When the parents get too old to take care of themselves, the son's family takes over and looks after their needs. Dying is a very natural process for the elderly. Their life is never prolonged by artificial measures for any reason. In fact, quite often some elderly people in Africa prefer not to be hospitalized, and make their wishes known regarding family affairs before they die.

The most touching and at the same time intriguing element about the wishes of the elders is that they leave their special blessings, skills or talents to a specific member of the family—someone who has been extremely close to the elder. African people are careful how they treat their elderly, so that they be blessed at the time of the passing of an elder.

Several generations live together, and the elderly spend

a great deal of time teaching the young the traditional ways of the clan. The elderly possess a storehouse of character-building stories, fine examples of adventure and mystery, peppered with words of wisdom all which they dispense to their attentive, young audience. Children and young adults alike honor and respect the older members of the family, seek their presence and build their growth and maturity on the lessons learned from them.

In my sub-tribe, the elderly and children often relate to each other as brothers and sisters because of our child-naming process. Traditionally, child naming is a privilege usually awarded to the oldest member of the paternal family. Babies are named after ancestors who have passed away— a custom which keeps the ancestor's good character alive. (Some tribes name children after living family members).

Children are named after their grandparents but not after their parents. The children are awarded the same respect as their namesake. For example, if the child is named after her mother, she is addressed as "mother" plus the chosen name with exactly the same reverence one would give one's own mother.

The interdependence of the African family can be quite an economical challenge in this day and age to some of its members, but the overall strength of this cultural distinction overweighs the negative aspects of being "too" closely knit.

African Wedding

On a bright sunny morning, in Chwele, a village in Western Kenya, the mood is charged with excitement. The air is filled with jubilant sounds from the beat of the wedding drums, which send their joyful message far and wide. Streams of villagers arrive, colorfully dressed in garments ranging from bright rainbow hues to muted earth tones, blending harmoniously with the land and the wild, cheering flowers along the paths and roadsides.

The people follow the sound of the drums and the robust aroma of food cooking which leads unerringly to the homestead of the bride. Weddings are usually celebrated in the month of December which is a hot and dry season, following the maize harvest. The bright sun gently releases rays of blessings. People's faces are bright with laughter and their spirits soar with joy. Brilliantly-hued, wild flowers reflect the generosity of nature and the vitality of life.The weather is comfortable and pleasant.

The groom approaches the village accompanied by his army of villagers like a conquering warrior. Indeed, he may have conquered the heart of the bride, but he has yet to win the vigilant hearts of the bride's villagers. Her people warn him of their wrath were he ever to mistreat their daughter, and they let him know they have brought her up the right way.

When a bride is given away in marriage, technically she is no longer a member of her birth family. She assumes the name of her husband's family and his clan. In spite of this transition, she is still looked after and protected by her blood relatives.

The bride remains discreetly tucked away in a quiet room where she is surrounded by honorable elder women of integrity, who skillfully pass on to her their age-old tidbits of marriage wisdom. The secrets of true womanhood and marriage are faithfully handed down to her. She knows the ways of womanhood, her responsibilities as a wife which includes the art of cooking. The seeds of love and endurance are sown in her heart. She is truly blessed by the elders' presence and their dedication to the young woman. The bridegroom is instructed in the same way by the male elders.

When she emerges from the room to face the expectant crowd and eager groom in the long-awaited ceremony, she seems transformed. She is the reigning queen of the day. She has become a novelty to the children. She walks on a bed of fragrant, bright wildflowers to meet her man. The flowers are lovingly sprinkled on her path by the delicate hands and happy hearts of younger sisters and cousins.

In the meantime, the men and young boys busy themselves with the final touches of the seating arrangements under a huge umbrella-like sycamore tree. To top the joyous mood, every kitchen in the bride's homestead simmers with delicious flavorful authentic cooking. Like busy bees, the women and young girls skillfully chop and peel, dice, braise and simmer, and taste the bursting flavors of chicken and beef curries, fragrant rice with ginger and groundnut (peanut), spicy sauce, sesame seed sauce, mashed bananas artistically wrapped in aroma-releasing banana leaves. What a picture!

A traditional wedding lasts for two days. On the first day, the festivities take place at the bride's home and the next day is spent celebrating at the groom's dwelling. These highly charged, intense events last from dawn through the night.

There is excitement in the air and the sounds of joyful visiting between the members of the communities. Among the traditional ceremonies, the gift-giving event is one of the most touching and memorable of the day.

The gift-giving song is performed by the circle of guests and calls upon different relatives — one group at a time. When the mother's side of the family is called in song to come forward and present their gifts, aunts and cousins form a joyful procession singing as they make their way. They offer their gifts in praise of the bride and groom. The gift-giving song continues until all the relatives have been called — an event that takes hours.

Each group of relatives usually presents practical gifts according to the traditions of the culture. The bride and groom are given just about everything to start a homestead of their own — from cutlery, kitchen utensils, bedding, furniture to livestock.

In the Luhya tribe the wedding ceremony is never complete without the singing of the traditional song "Mwana wa mbeli in Sikhoyelo" — "The first child in a family is a child of joy." This song casts a magical spell on the singers and they keep dancing on and on with seemingly inexhaustible energy. But the element that ties all the facets of this traditional wedding ceremony together, of course, is the wonderful food which has been so lovingly prepared and is so joyfully shared.

The love and care — the enormous emotional investment — that both the community and family expend on behalf of the young couple throughout their courtship and in their marriage, may well be the reason traditional marriages rarely break up, but thrive on the generous interaction between the young and the "old."

While we are on the subject of "old," I would like to mention just how much the East African community depends on the elders, how they are respected and revered. The old are the wise ones and rather than being considered a bother, they are the foundation of their clans' emotional and ethical well being, and the source of knowledge, traditions and ancient customs. The elders are indeed valuable. Without their guidance, new generations would go into the world with empty hearts and vacant souls.

Kwanzaa - A Celebration

Kwanzaa is a seven-day holiday and was introduced to the United States by Dr. Manlana Karenga, founder and chairman of the Black Nationalist Organization "U.S." *Kwanzaa* is a cultural holiday recognized by African Americans to demonstrate the concept of the Seven Principles *(nguzo saba)* which are based on the African family value system. The meaning of these principles was taken away from African Americans by the ordeal of slavery, and colonialism further eroded African principles. They are now being recaptured to give these people (especially the children) a sense of positive African values.

The word *"kwanzaa"* comes from the Swahili word,

kwanza, which means first and is part of the phrase *"matun-da ya kwanza"* (first fruits). The biggest cultural celebrations in Africa usually happen around harvest time. Weddings take place right after harvest time when there is plenty to eat and a time to give thanks for the harvests. The seven principles of *kwanzaa* stem from the "eating family circle."

Once one has learned the values of sharing and belonging through the eating circle experience, then one is able to more fully participate in the seven principles with a heightened community spirit and a sense of unity. One of the *kwanzaa* symbols is *zawadi* which is a Kiswahili word that means "gift." The giving of gifts part of the celebration is the highlight for the children. In traditional Africa, materialism did not exist, even at Christmas time. Since there was so little to give in terms of material gifts, African families gave to each other in many different ways. They still give of themselves to each other every day because that is all they have at times.

When an elder tells a story to a child, he blesses that youngster with memories no one can take ever away. When certain words of wisdom are used to demonstrate a cultural value to a child, that too is a gift he'll have forever. The time the elders spend with the young ones to teach them time-honored lessons of life is a great gift in itself. The time children spend making their own toys and dolls for each other is a gift. The most precious gifts are those of time, effort, sharing, encouragement, respect and belonging. During the *kwanzaa* celebration, children are encouraged to create their own decorations and gifts which symbolize cultural values to exchange with each other and not to expect to be given a gift as in the western tradition.

The seven principles of kwanzaa are:

1. December 26 - Umoja (oo-moe-jah) Unity.
    To strive and maintain unity in the family, community, nation and race.
2. December 27 - Kujichangulia (koo-jee-cha-ngoo-lee-ah).
    Self Determination. To define ourselves, name ourselves, create for ourselves and speak for ourselves, instead of being defined, named, created for and spoken for by others.
3. December 28 - Ujima (oo-jee-mah) Collective Work and Responsibility.
    To build and maintain our community together and to make our sisters' and brothers' problems our problems, and solve them together.
4. December 29 - Ujamaa (oo-jah-mah) Cooperative Economics.
    To build and maintain our own stores, shops and other businesses and profit from them together.
5. December 30 - Nia (nee-ah) Purpose.
    To make as our collective vocation the building and developing of our community in order to restore our people to their traditional greatness.
6. December 31 - Kuumba (koo-oom-bah) Creativity.
    To always do as much as we can, in the way we can, in order to leave our community more beautiful and beneficial than when we inherited it.
7. January 1 - Imani (ee-mah-nee) Faith.
    To believe with all our hearts in our people, our parents, our teachers, our leaders and the righteousness and victory of our struggle.

All of the symbols for *kwanzaa* are:
- straw mat *(mkeka)*.
- candle holder *(kinara)*.
- seven candles *(mishumaa)*.
- fruits and vegetables *(mazao)*.
- ears of corn *(vibunzi)*.
- gifts *(zawadi)* and .
- cup *(kikombe)*.

Celebrating one's culture gives one a sense of identity and the spirit of belonging. To appreciate what might happen in the future we need to know our past.

The Heart Of Africa

Affectionate and kind is the African child,
While Africa's soul is both gentle and wild.
Women are born of a love that is strong,
Admired be men in words and in song.

She tackles her world with energy and drive,
And life around her never ceases to thrive.
She has little time for leisure and play,
But her spirit is happy, her heart is gay.
Singing like a weaver, she does her chores with a song,
And still has a smile when everything goes wrong.

Like an architect she builds her family foundation
Far beyond the horizons of her imagination.
Her life is dedicated to those she loves,
And the earth, the land and the song of the doves.
Her offspring drink deep from her cup of affection
And stand by her side in times of affliction.

Her magnificent heart embraces all things,
The flowers, the children and creatures with wings.
Her strength is the heartbeat of African life,
She's the teacher, the mother, the friend and the wife

She is the pillar of virtue in her African home,
The beacon of light for those who did roam.
She is a hundred times blessed with a sense of survival,
She is the vigor and the power behind value revival.
She is the hope and the backbone of true African living,
The real source of all caring, sharing and giving.

    To my mother - Assanta Sana!

    Grace

Listing Of Recipes

❤ = AHA = Meets the American Heart Association guidelines.

Ugali
Maize Meal Mash

4 cups water
4 cups maize flour (yellow or white)

1. In a deep pan bring water to boil and reduce heat to medium high.
2. Using a flat cooking stick *(mwiko)* or a regular wooden spoon, slowly stir the flour into the boiling water a little at a time.
3. Stir constantly to minimize lumping.
4. Keep pressing the lumps until they are all out.
5. Let *ugali* cook without stirring for about two minutes or so then turn it over.
6. Repeat this several times for about 10 minutes.
7. It should turn out as a stiff dough.
8. Serve on a flat dinner plate and smooth the edges immediately with another dinner plate.
9. *Ugali* should be eaten with a curry dish plus any vegetable.

This dish is the most commonly used among all the staple foods in East Africa especially in Kenya. It is a stiff porridge. Africans generally do a lot of manual work and this dish is fairly high in calories to satisfy their hunger. After you eat *ugali,* you are not hungry for a very long time. This is an extremely popular dish among the Luo and Luhya tribes in western Kenya. The best way to learn to make this dish is to actually watch someone else do it first because timing on adding the flour is very critical. Nutritionally, *ugali* is a high-energy food — complex carbohydrate.

"If a new hoe needs to know the condition of the earth, let it ask the old hoe."

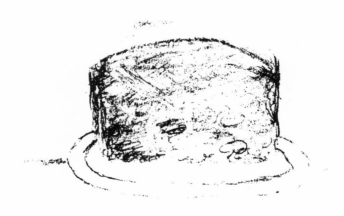

Wimbi Ugali
Millet Flour Ugali

4 cups water
4 cups millet flour (powdery light brown)

1. In a deep pan bring water to boil.
2. Reduce heat to medium.
3. Using a flat wooden cooking stick *(mwiko)* or regular wooden spoon, slowly stir the flour into the boiling water a little at a time.
4. Stir constantly as you add the flour to minimize lumping.
5. Watch out for bubbling and reduce heat if mixture is bubbling too much.
6. Keep pressing the lumps with wooden spoon until they are all out.
7. Turn occasionally for another 5 minutes.
8. It should turn out to be a fairly stiff dough.
9. Serve on a flat dinner plate, let stand for a minute then smooth the edges with another dinner plate.
10. Serve with any curry meat and vegetable.
    Serves six.

Wimbi Ugali is not as popular as Ugali. Since it requires a lot of work from the time the millet is planted to the time the flour is ready for consumption, it is reserved for special occasions and celebrations in some African communities.

Kenyan medical experts recommend its use for patients with digestive problems. This particular grain is easier to digest than cornmeal, but it takes a more skilled and experienced hand to prepare Wimbi Ugali than its cousin, the maize Ugali.

Preparation for this meal is best learned by watching someone who knows how to cook it.

As a complex carbohydrate, millet is a good source of certain minerals.

"One stick of firewood can't build a fire."

Ndizi
Mashed Bananas

10 almost ripe green bananas
2 cups of water
Pinch of salt (optional)
1/2 teaspoon margarine (optional)

1. Peel and wash bananas.
2. Chop each banana in fairly large pieces.
3. In a deep pot, bring bananas to boil in water and a little salt if desired.
4. Reduce heat to low medium and cook for 5 to 10 minutes until soft.
5. Drain all water.
6. Add margarine and mash bananas with a wooden spoon or potato masher.
7. Serve with curry and vegetable.
        Serves four.

This is a popular staple dish in all of East Africa—especially in Uganda and Western Kenya. It is a "light" meal for people who are not in excellent health, and is well liked by the elderly because it is easy to digest, and a good provider of potassium. In rural areas, bananas are mashed, wrapped in green banana leaves, and left to steep for a few hours near the cooking fire. With time, the leaves release their sweet aroma into the bananas. The result is a delicious treat. It is that special taste and aroma which makes Ndizi a popular dish at wedding ceremonies.

Should you find yourself in an area in Africa where Ndizi is prepared, don't miss the opportunity to try it because of its special aroma.

"Young birds don't know when bananas are ripe."

Mchuzi Wa Ndizi
Curried Bananas

5 green bananas (almost ripe)
1 small onion or 2 stems green onion, chopped
1/2 to 1 teaspoon margarine
1 teaspoon curry
Pinch of salt (optional)
1/2 cup water

1. Peel bananas, wash and chop.
2. Saute onions in margarine
3. Add bananas and stir.
4. Add curry and stir until well mixed.
5. Add pinch of salt if desired.
6. Add water, bring to boil and simmer for 5 minutes or until cooked.
7. Serve as a side dish with rice, beans and vegetable.
    Serves ten.

Although bananas are a traditional food, this recipe has an East Indian flavor due to the use of curry, and is served more in cities than in rural areas. Children raised in urban areas prefer to eat their bananas this way.

Bananas provide potassium.

"If you don't know any proverbs, you have no ancestors."

Ndizi Karanga
Fried Bananas

5 green bananas (almost ripe)
1 tablespoon curry
2 tablespoons flour
Pinch of salt
Oil for frying

1. Peel bananas and wash.
2. Dry bananas thoroughly with kitchen paper towel.
3. Slice bananas in half crosswise then in half lengthwise.
4. Mix curry, flour and salt in a plastic bag. Add banana pieces to bag and shake to cover bananas with mixture.
5. Heat a little oil in a frying pan. Fry bananas on both sides until brown.
6. Serve warm with curry dish and any vegetable of choice.
    Serves ten.

Bananas are a popular traditional food. Fried bananas are mainly eaten in the urban environment, but are expensive because they are grown in the country and brought to the city by small peasant farmers who need money for children's school fees.

"Catch a bull by the horns, a man by his words."

Ndizi Na Mnazi
Bananas In Coconut

6 green bananas (almost ripe)
1 to 2 teaspoons margarine
1 large onion, chopped
1 medium tomato, chopped
Salt and pepper to taste
1 cup coconut milk

1. Peel and slice (crosswise) the bananas.
2. Saute the onion until tender
3. Add tomato and sliced bananas and mix.
4. Add seasoning, coconut milk and mix.
5. Cook for 5 to 10 minutes until tender.
   Serves four.

Coconut is mostly used in cooking by people who live in the coastal areas for added flavor. Coconuts are fairly high in saturated fat and should not be used in the daily diet.

Bananas are high in potassium.

"The person who isn't hungry says 'the coconut shell is hard.'"

Wali Wa Tangausi
Ginger Rice

4 cups jasmine rice (white)
8 cups water
1/4 teaspoon salt (optional)
1 tablespoon margarine
1 tablespoon fresh ginger, grated
1 medium onion, chopped
1/2 teaspoon curry (optional)
1 cup boiled valencia peanuts (optional) or
1 cup boiled mung beans (optional)

1. In a deep sauce pan, bring water to boil.
2. Wash rice.
3. To boiling water, add 1/2 tablespoon margarine, salt and rice.
4. On medium high heat, bring rice and water to boil then reduce heat to lower medium heat.
5. Cook until all water is absorbed.
6. When rice is about cooked, saute chopped onion and grated ginger in remaining margarine. Add curry if desired.
7. Add cooked rice (little by little) to onions and ginger and stir fry until rice is well mixed with ginger and onion, add groundnuts (optional) or mung beans (optional).
8. Serve hot with any meat curry or beans and a vegetable dish.
        Serves eight to ten.

This fragrant, delicious rice is prepared for guests and for weddings, birthdays, family reunions and other celebrations. Rice is used mostly in urban and suburban areas, and was first introduced to East Africa by East Indians and early traders along the coast. Brown rice is not popular in East Africa because most of it has to be imported.

White rice contains small amounts of phosphorous, protein and potassium, and is nutritionally most beneficial when eaten with beans.

"Plant where you are and you will never be hungry."

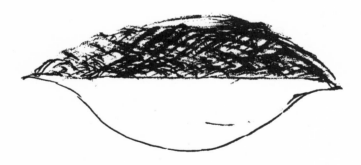

Wali Wa Mnazi
Coconut Rice

4 cups jasmine rice (white)
8 cups water
1/4 teaspoon salt (optional)
1/2 tablespoon margarine
2 tablespoons grated coconut

1. In a deep pan, bring water to boil.
2. Wash rice.
3. To boiling water, add rice, coconut, margarine and salt.
4. On medium high heat, bring rice and water to boil then reduce heat to lower medium.
5. Cook until all water is absorbed.
6. Serve hot with meat curry or beans plus vegetable.
      Serves eight to ten.

Since coconuts are grown in coastal regions of East Africa, their use is more common in that area. This is a delicious dish with a delicate flavor when properly prepared.

The nutritional value of rice is enhanced when served with beans.

"You will never pick a pepper from a lemon tree."

Viazi Kienyeji
Sweet Potatoes

3 large sweet potatoes
2 cups water
1/4 teaspoon salt (optional)
1 teaspoon margarine

1. Peel potatoes and chop them in medium size pieces.
2. In a deep pan, put potatoes, water and salt.
3. Bring contents to boil and reduce heat to medium.
4. Boil until soft (10 to 15 minutes).
5. Drain all water.
6. Put margarine over all the potatoes and let it melt.
7. Serve hot with meat curry or beans plus vegetables.
   Can also be eaten cold with tea of coffee.
   Serves eight.

Introduced by Portuguese traders, the sweet potato has been a traditional staple in East Africa for over 100 years. It is widely used, because it can be harvested in just three months after planting. Sweet potatoes make a tasty snack, a tasty side dish and can be served hot or cold.

Easy to prepare, sweet potatoes are an energy-producing food and rich in vitamin A.

"When the food is good, people are silent."

Viazi
Irish Potatoes

10 large Irish potatoes
1 medium onion, chopped
1/3 medium bunch dhania (cilantro), chopped
1/2 teaspoon garlic, grated
1/2 teaspoon ginger, grated
1 teaspoon margarine or vegetable oil
1 cup water
Salt or seasoned salt to taste (optional)

1. Peel and wash potatoes.
2. Cut potatoes in medium pieces.
4. Saute onions, cilantro, garlic and ginger in margarine or oil then add potatoes to the mixture.
5. Add water to potatoes. Add salt to taste. 6. Bring contents to boil and reduce heat to medium low. Cook potatoes for about 10 minutes or until soft.
7. Serve with meat curry or beans plus vegetables.
	Serves eight.

   Although the Irish potato is not an African food, it has become a staple in the East African home. Potatoes are widely grown by both large and small farm operations, and are one of the most traded commodities on the open markets. Potatoes can be used in many ways, but are especially good and filling when prepared in stews.

   The Irish potato is the most multi- nutrient food in existence, since it has vitamins, minerals, carbohydrates and protein.

   "Dine on the big fish first, the little ones later."

Maindi Mbichi
Green or Sweet Corn

4 cobs of sweet corn, fresh
Water to boil
Margarine (optional)

1. In a deep pan, place corn and water together and bring to boil. Reduce heat to medium and boil for 10 to 15 minutes or until cooked.
2. Africans do not eat their corn with butter or margarine, but you may do so if you wish. Try eating it without!
3. Serve as a snack, dessert or side dish.
    Serves four.

This is the most favorite snack on the whole African continent. The corn grown in Africa is harder than that produced in the United States. You can pop its kernels off the cob line by line by using your thumb (khubulungula).

Corn on the cob is usually eaten last when included in a meal. We used to play a game when eating corn we called "tax sharing." The game encourages children to share with each other. Whoever finishes his piece of corn first goes to the next person still eating, and makes a gesture that resembles the putting on make-believe handcuffs.

The first person informs the slower eater that she was being arrested for not paying taxes and is collecting the kernels in payment, until all the corn is gone.

Sweet corn is a good source of energy, while yellow corn contains vitamin A.

"Don't say you have corn until it's in the measure."

Samusa
Wrapped Meat or Vegetable Filling

1 pound ground beef or ground chicken or
   3 cups boiled mung beans for vegetarian
2 teaspoons curry powder
1/2 clove garlic, grated or pressed
Salt and black pepper to taste (optional)
1/2 bunch cilantro
1 medium yellow onion, chopped
8 ounces frozen French cut green beans, chopped
1 green pepper, chopped
1/2 medium size savoy cabbage, chopped
1 cup cheese, grated
10 medium tortillas or 25 won ton wrappers
36 fluid ounces vegetable oil (traditional method)

1. Saute beef or chicken stirring frequently to prevent lumping. Saute until all visible fat is melted. Or saute boiled mung beans.
2. Drain all fat.
3. Add seasonings. Add onion and stir until cooked. Add the rest of the vegetables, green beans first. Cook a little before adding the rest. Cabbage should be added last. Stir mixture together for next minute or so. Do not over-cook vegetables.
    Contemporary wrapping method:
4. Spread 2 tablespoonfuls of mixture on 2/3 of a tortilla and roll. Sprinkle grated cheese on the remaining 1/3 of tortilla and complete rolling.
5. To melt cheese, place in conventional oven on warm

(200 degrees) for 10 minutes or microwave for 1 minute. If refrigerated, microwave for 2 minutes or in warm oven for 30 minutes. Small size tortillas are great for parties.

Traditional wrapping method:

4. In a deep pan heat vegetable oil.

5. Place 2 tablespoons of mixture on half of won ton wrapper diagonally.

6. Brush all edges with a little plain water. Fold won ton wrapper in a diagonal shape and press edges together until they are completely sealed. The wrapper should be dry on the outside before frying.

7. Deep fry in heated oil until golden brown. Remove from oil. Immediately drain on absorbent kitchen paper towel and let cool.

Samusa is consumed all over the world, and is known by different names. It is popular in India, the Middle East and in Africa. It was introduced to the East African region by people from India at the turn of the century. It is a favorite dish for natives and is enjoyed by western peoples.

The traditional wrapping method is used by Indians, Africans and Middle Eastern people. A new wrapping method was created by the *African Women Harambee Association* of Portland, Oregon to accommodate people who no longer indulge in deep fried foods, and has been a hit. We discovered that this method saves a lot of preparation time and lowers the cost of ingredients.

Samusas are usually prepared for guests or for parties. Various size wrappers may also be used. This is a healthy recipe and a full meal in itself. Use as much of the vegetable mixture you wish.

This dish is an excellent source of protein and carbohydrates.

Mchuzi Wa Kuku
Chicken Curry

1 whole chicken
1 large onion or 1 bunch green onions, chopped
1 teaspoon garlic, grated or pressed
1 teaspoon ginger, grated
1 green bell pepper, chopped
1 to 2 tablespoons vegetable oil
1 heaping tablespoon curry powder
1/8 teaspoon black pepper (optional)
1 can tomato sauce (6 ounces) or 2 large tomatoes,
    chopped
2 cups water
Salt or seasoned salt to taste
1 small bunch *dhania* (cilantro), chopped or 1/2 tea
    spoon cumin seed

1. Cut up chicken, skin and wash.
2. In a deep pan, saute onions, garlic, ginger, bell pepper
in oil. Add curry and black pepper.
3. Add chicken to mixture and stir until well mixed.
4. Add tomatoes or tomato sauce to chicken.
5. Add water and salt to taste.
6. Add either cilantro or cumin seed.
7. Bring contents to boil and reduce heat to simmer.
8. Simmer chicken for 20 minutes or until cooked.
9. Serve hot with any of the dishes from main dish section
plus vegetable.
    Serves six to eight.

This is a special dish in most East African communities served at special occasions. Preparation of this chicken curry dish announces the fact that a special guest will be sharing the meal, or that there is a reason for a celebration. In the family circle, the guest always gets the largest choicest piece of chicken. This gesture signifies that the visitor is indeed the guest of honor, and is intended to make him feel acknowledged and accepted in the family's home.

You may add carrots and Irish potatoes to this dish to stretch it. If you add carrots and potatoes, add an extra cup of water during cooking because potatoes absorb more water as they cook.

"Don't allow a hungry chicken to guard your corn."

Mchuzi Wa Nyama Ya Ngombe
Beef Curry

1 pound stewing beef or chuck roast, cut up
1 to 2 tablespoons vegetable oil
1 large onion or 1 bunch green onions, chopped
1 teaspoon garlic, grated or pressed
1 green bell pepper, chopped
1 small bunch *dhania* (cilantro), chopped or
   1/4 teaspoon cumin seed
1 tablespoon curry
Salt to taste
1/8 teaspoon black pepper (optional)
1 can tomato sauce (6 ounces) or
   2 large tomatoes, chopped
2 cups water

1. Cut up beef and wash if need be.
2. In a deep pan saute onions, garlic, green pepper and cilantro or cumin seed. Add salt and pepper and curry.
3. Add beef to contents and stir thoroughly.
4. Add tomato sauce or chopped tomatoes and mix.
5. Add water and stir contents. If more liquid is desired you may add more water and salt accordingly.
6. Bring contents to boil and reduce heat to simmer. Simmer for 30 to 45 minutes or until beef is softly cooked.
7. Serve hot with rice or any main dish item and vegetables.
   Serves six to eight.

The use of beef is not common in rural areas, and is considered a treat for guests and is used in celebration of special events, such as wedding, family reunion, dowry ceremony, etc. Sometimes the meat is dried over an open fire (barbeque) to preserve it for later use since there is no refrigeration in rural areas. Simmered in curry and spices, the dried variety is better tasting than fresh meat prepared in the same manner.

In order to stretch this dish, it is common practice to add vegetables such as *sukuma wiki* (collard greens) or cabbage in order to feed more people with the same amount of meat. Meat is a good source of protein, but since beef is rarely eaten, beans remain the main source for protein in the native diet.

"If you eat with a cunning person, hold a long spoon."

Mchuzi Wa Nyama Ya Ngombe Na Sukuma Wiki
Beef With Collard Greens

1 pound minced meat (hamburger meat)
2 bunches fresh *sukuma wiki* (collard greens)
1 bunch green onions or 1 medium yellow
    onion, chopped
1 to 2 teaspoons curry powder
Salt or seasoning salt to taste
Pinch of black pepper
1 can tomato sauce (6 ounces) or 1 medium
    tomato, chopped
1 can water (6 ounces)

1. Chop and wash *sukuma wiki.*
2. Saute meat in a deep pan until all fat has melted from the beef.
3. Drain as much fat as possible out of the meat.
4. Add onions, curry powder, pepper and salt, stir then add *sukuma wiki.*
5. Stir thoroughly to mix and let cook for a couple of minutes.
6. Add tomato sauce or tomatoes and stir.
7. Add water and stir.
8. Bring contents to boil and simmer for 10 minutes.
9. Serve hot with *ugali* or rice.
        Serves 10 or more.

This is a dish most often prepared in urban and suburban areas. Minced meat is not available in most rural areas because the machinery for grinding the meat is not available. This recipe is an excellent way of stretching meat. Some families use more vegetables in this dish than suggested in this recipe. The end result is a vegetable dish flavored with a little minced meat which makes it a healthy meal.

You may substitute beef with ground turkey or chicken. The collard greens can also be substituted with frozen or fresh spinach, or spinach combined with cabbage. Try different leafy vegetables for this recipe until you find your favorite.

This meal provides protein (depends on amount of meat used), fiber and calcium.

"A poor cook doesn't enjoy guests."

Mchuzi Wa Nyama Na Njugu
Meat with Groundnut Sauce

1 whole chicken
1 tablespoon vegetable oil for cooking
1 large onion, chopped
2 large fresh tomatoes, chopped
3 tablespoons tomato paste (optional)
Salt or seasoned salt to taste
2 tablespoons peanut butter (groundnut paste)
1 to 2 cups water

1. Chop, skin and wash chicken.
2. Saute onions in oil.
3. Add chopped tomatoes.
4. Add chicken and salt.
5. Add tomato past if desired.
6. Add peanut butter and mix all ingredients together.
7. Add water.
8. Bring to boil and simmer for 20 minutes.
9. Serve with rice or Ugali or any carbohydrate main dish plus vegetable.
   Serves 8 to 10.

This is a more traditional way of cooking chicken in my country. Groundnut paste and sim sim paste (sesame seed paste) have been used as food flavoring in African cooking for many years. Since it takes time to prepare both pastes, they are considered a delicacy, and are used sparingly in some parts of East Africa. The oils from groundnuts and sim sim are the "good" oils which lower cholesterol in the body.

This flavorful dish contains lots of protein.

It is served at weddings and as well as family and community celebrations.

"Don't plant groundnuts when baboons are watching."

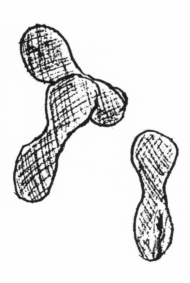

Kuku Mabaki
Leftover Chicken

margarine or oil for cooking
2 cups chopped left over chicken
1 medium onion, chopped
1 teaspoon ginger, grated
1 teaspoon curry powder
Salt or seasoning salt to taste
Pinch of black pepper
1 chopped green bell pepper
3 grated carrots
2 cups shredded cabbage
1/2 cup milk (optional)

1. In a large frying pan, saute chicken, onions and ginger.
2. Add curry, salt and black pepper.
3. Add all chopped vegetables and stir until all ingredients are well mixed.
4. At this point you may add milk, bring to boil and simmer for a minute.
5. You may omit milk and cook contents on medium heat for 2 to 3 minutes. Serve while vegetables are still crunchy.
    Serves 6.

This is a dish I created once, because I was in a hurry. In spite of the haste with which this meal was prepared, I was pleased with the results.

Vegetables can be varied according to availability and personal preference. If milk is used in this recipe, add 1 tsp of all purpose flower for thickening.

"You will harvest whatever seeds you plant."

Githeri Na Njugu
Beans and Peanuts

2 cups dried red beans
1/2 pound minced meat (hamburger meat) or
   ground chicken or turkey
1 large onion, chopped
1 teaspoon ginger, grated
1 teaspoon garlic, grated or pressed
6 carrots, diced
1 to 2 tablespoons curry powder
1/8 teaspoon black pepper
Salt or seasoning salt to taste
1 cup boiled groundnuts (peanuts) (optional)
3 cups sweet corn (maize)
1 can tomato or mushroom soup
2 cans tomato sauce (6 ounce cans)
6 to 12 ounces water

1. Soak beans in cold water overnight or for an hour in warm water before cooking time. Boil beans until cooked.
2. In a deep *sufuria* (sauce pan) saute meat and drain all extra fat out.
3. Add onions, ginger, garlic and carrots and stir.
4. Add curry powder, black pepper and salt and stir.
5. Add beans, groundnuts and sweet corn and stir.
6. Add tomato sauce, soup and water and bring to boil.
7. Reduce heat to simmer and cook for 30 minutes.
8. This is a complete meal but may be served as a side dish.

   Serves 10 or more.

This dish is made in several parts of East Africa, and is prepared in a variety of ways and given different names. This recipe is the one most commonly prepared in Kenya, and represents the most staple dish among the Kikuyu and related tribes. Their version of this dish is made with Irish potatoes. This is a meal served in almost all boarding schools in Kenya. The school version is not as palatable as the home-made one because it is prepared in such large quantities and bears the stamp of institutional food.

The high school I attended is located among the Kikuyu people, and prided itself in having the best *githeri* cooks.

This wholesome, hearty meal is often eaten after a hard day's work, and does not require complementary side dishes. A bowl of *githeri* and fruit salad is all you need, since it is a great source of protein and carbohydrates.

"Even in time of famine, there is dew on the grass."

Mukenye
Beans and Mashed Sweet Potatoes

1 cup dried kidney beans
3 large sweet potatoes , peeled and chopped
Salt or seasoned salt to taste
1 large onion, chopped (optional)
1 cup maize (sweet corn)
1 tablespoon margarine
Water to cook.

1. Soak beans overnight in cold water or for one hour in warm water.
2. Cook beans until very soft.
3. Cook potatoes in salted (optional) water until soft.
4. In a deep *sufuria* (sauce pan) saute onions in margarine.
5. Add beans, and potatoes to onions. Add a little more salt if desired.
6. Mash potatoes and beans until well mixed and mashed.
7. Add sweet corn to contents and mix well.
8. Serve hot with vegetables. May be served hot or cold with Kenyan tea.
        Serves 10 or more.

Mukenye is a Luhya word for this dish, and is most popular among the Luhya people of Western Kenya. There are several versions of *Mukenye* due to the varieties of beans used in its preparation. It is often eaten for breakfast accompanied by tea or coffee — especially by young people. *Mukenye* is served as a side dish and is a good source of protein and energy. It is a traditional food, liked for its filling qualities after a hard day's work, and it also a favorite snack.

"To ask twice is better than not understanding."

Maharagwe Meusi
Black Beans and Sweet Corn

2 cups black beans, dried
2 cups *maize* (sweet corn)
1 cup boiled groundnuts (peanuts)
1 tablespoon margarine
Salt or seasoning salt to taste

1. Do not soak beans, the earthy rich flavor gets diluted.
2. Check beans for debris and wash them.
3. Cook beans for 1 to 1-1/2 hour adding water as needed.
4. Drain all water out of cooked beans.
5. Add sweet corn and boiled peanuts.
6. Add margarine and salt to taste.
7. Mix contents thoroughly and leave on simmer before serving.
8. Serve hot with rice as a side dish.
     Serves 10 or more.

While this is not the most inviting looking dish, black beans have a most distinct, earthy taste people find hard to resist. Most people who frown at the look of those unappealing beans, change their minds once they have tasted them. It is one of my favorite bean dishes, and so easy to prepare.

Cook for recommended time or until tender.

This dish is a rich source of protein and potassium.

"Looking at food doesn't satisfy the stomach."

Mchuzi Wa Ndengu
Mung Bean Stew

2 cups dried mung beans
1 teaspoon margarine
1 large onion, chopped
2 medium fresh tomatoes, chopped
1 teaspoon garlic, grated or pressed
Salt or seasoning salt to taste
Pinch black pepper (optional)
1 to 2 teaspoons curry powder
1 cup water
1 beef or chicken bullion cube

1. Check beans for debris.
2. Boil beans in a *sufuria* (deep sauce pan) until soft.
3. While beans are cooking chop onions and tomatoes.
4. Drain all water out of cooked beans.
5. Saute onions in margarine then add tomatoes and all seasonings.
6. Add water and bullion cube, bring to boil and reduce heat to simmer. Simmer for 3 to 5 minutes.
7. Serve hot with rice or chapati.
Serves 10.

This is a delicious dish with a distinctive flavor. It is not commonly eaten in rural parts, but is a popular bean dish in urban and suburban areas. Many Americans have never seen or eaten mung beans, while mung bean sprouts are known and used among the American people. The bean itself is small and dull greenish in color. Mung beans cook much faster than other beans. You will find mung beans in health food stores or Asian markets.

Mung beans are known to have a richer supply of protein and potassium than some of their cousins. Their sprouts are rich in potassium.

"One who has eaten doesn't make a fire for the hungry."

Ndengu Na Viazi Kienyeji
Mung Beans and Sweet Potatoes

2 cups dried mung beans
3 large sweet potatoes
1 large onion, chopped
1 tablespoon margarine
Salt or seasoning salt to taste

1. Check beans for debris.
2. Boil in *sufuria* (deep sauce pan) until soft
3. Boil potatoes until soft.
4. Saute onion in margarine.
5. Add cooked mung beans and potatoes.
6. Add salt to taste.
7. Mash mixture until potatoes are very smooth.
8. Serve hot with curry plus vegetable. May be served as a snack with tea or coffee.
    Serves 10.

This is a most traditional way of cooking mung beans. It is used in the same way as the recipe for beans and sweet potatoes (page 92). Mung beans are not as popular in rural areas as they used to be. Preparing mung beans for human consumption is labor intensive.

See more information on page 96, Mung bean stew.

"One hand can't tie a bundle."

Lentils

2 cups dried lentils
2 cups carrots, sliced
1 large onion, chopped
1 tablespoon margarine
1 teaspoon garlic, grated or pressed
1 teaspoon ginger, grated
1 to 2 teaspoons curry powder
pinch of black pepper
Salt or seasoning salt to taste
1 can tomato sauce (6 ounces) or 1 large tomato,
    chopped
12 ounces of water

1. Check lentils for debris and wash.
2. Saute onions and carrots in margarine in deep pan.
3. Add seasonings.
4. Add lentils and mix.
5. Add tomato sauce or tomatoes and water.
6. Bring to boil and simmer for 10 minutes or until well cooked.
7. Serve with rice or chapatis.
    Serves 10 or more.

This is a typical East Asian or Mid-Eastern dish. It has been served in East Africa for so long that it is considered one of the authentic African dishes. It is mainly eaten in the urban and suburban areas.

Lentils have a distinct taste but are delicious and rich in phosphorus and potassium.

"A little axe can cut down a big tree."

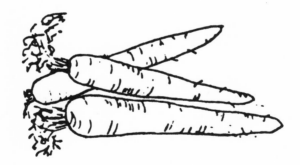

Irio
Mashed Irish Potatoes, Beans and Vegetables

    1 to 2 tablespoons margarine
    5 large Irish potatoes, peeled and chopped
    1 cup red beans, cooked
    2 green bananas (almost ripe) optional
    1 package frozen chopped spinach (10 ounces),
       thawed, or fresh spinach
    Salt or seasoning salt to taste
    Water for cooking
    1 cup maize (sweet corn)

1. Prepare and chop all vegetables.
2. In a *sufuria* (deep sauce pan) saute onion until soft.
3. Add potatoes, beans and stir for about 5 minutes.
4. Add bananas and stir.
5. Add spinach and stir.
6. Add salt and water to cook.
7. Cook until soft then mash mixture thoroughly.
8. Add maize and mix well.
9. Let simmer for 3 to 5 minutes.
10. Serve hot with curry and vegetables.
       Serves 10 or more.

Irio can be prepared in many different ways. The above recipe is only one of the several versions for this tasty dish which originated from the Kikuyu people who have perfected its taste. One of my sisters, Elizabeth, makes the best *Irio*. When we visit with each other, she treats us to her famous version of preparing Irio.

In the spring of 1994 she came to visit us in Portland. After the children had acquainted her with our city's bus system, she asked matter-of-factly what bus line would take her to *Fred Meyer* shopping center.

One evening we came home from work and were greeted by the most delicious, but familiar aroma. I was puzzled because I didn't have the ingredients for cooking *Irio* in the house. But my sister simply had taken the bus to *Fred Meyer.* On her way back, she had gotten off two stops earlier than she should have since she was not familiar yet with our area. She had to walk the rest of the way lugging a heavy shopping bag — uphill all the way. She had cooked a surprise dinner for us, and served us her delicious *irio.* Her adventure of shopping by herself made the dinner even more special.

Irio is a good source of potassium and phosphorus. Pumpkin leaves can be used instead of spinach.

"Pleasantries and compliments are soon forgotten, criticisms and insults are long remembered."

Mandazi
Donut-like Fried Bread

4 cups all purpose flour
2 level teaspoons baking powder
2 tablespoons margarine
1/4 teaspoon masala (powdered mixed spices) or
    any one of the following spices: cinnamon,
    cardamom, all spice, ginger.
1 cup sugar
1 egg
1/3 cup milk
2 cups warm water
Vegetable oil for cooking.

1. Sift flour and baking powder together.
2. Rub margarine into the flour with finger-tips until smooth.
3. Add spice to flour and mix. Add sugar to flour and mix.
4. Beat egg, milk and water together. Little by little add water mixture into the flour and stir slowly with a wooden spoon until you have a semi-sticky dough.
5. Knead dough with hands until it is smooth and not sticky (pizza-like dough).
6. Heat oil in a deep pan until hot. Test temperature with a small piece of dough, if it cooks, then oil is ready.
7. Roll dough to 1/4 to 1/2 inch thick. Cut with dinner knife in desired sizes and shapes.
8. Deep fry in hot but not burning oil until golden brown.
9. Serve hot or cold with Kenyan spicy tea or coffee.
    Servings 10 or more.

Mandazis as we know them in East Africa are a universal food simply known by different names in various parts of the world. They are not a traditional food in East Africa, yet they have been around for close to a century. Mandazis are similar to donuts in the western world. We prepare them less sweet and they are more chewy and drier in consistency. Mandazis can be made in different flavors, are eaten for breakfast, make a popular snack food and are quick to prepare.

Most East African families can whip them up in just a few minutes to accompany a cup of tea or coffee for unexpected guests. They are extremely popular with children and are mainly an energy food.

"Awe and wonder are everywhere, if you open your eyes."

Flaky Chapatis
Fried Bread

4 cups all purpose flour
1/8 to 1/4 teaspoon salt
1 tablespoon margarine
1-1/3 cups warm water
Oil for cooking

1. Add salt to flour and lightly mix.
2. Add margarine and rub it into flour with finger tips until flour is smooth.
3. Make well in center of flour and pour in half the water. Mix slowly with a wooden spoon adding rest of water little by little until dough is firm but soft.
4. Knead the dough with your hands (adding a little flour if necessary) until it's smooth.
5. Divide dough in 8 balls. Roll each ball into a circle, rub the circle with a little oil, fold from one end and roll it with your hands into a long layered piece of dough.
6. Stretch and fold it into a wheel-like shape.
7. Roll out each piece of dough into a circular shape (about 6 to 8 inches diameter).
8. In a frying pan, fry each side of the circle on medium heat until golden brown in some areas.
9. Serve hot or cold with curry dish plus vegetable.
Serves 8.

Chapati is a flat lightly fried bread made from wheat flour. This is an East Indian dish which was introduced to East Africa in the early 1900s. It is a popular dish among young people, and is a winner with every guest. It is mostly served in urban areas where wheat flour is more readily available. Because *Chapati* is fried in oil, it has lots of calories, and takes time to prepare

Drink lots and lots of water after you have eaten *Chapati* to aid the digestive process. This is an energy food and has only minimal (other) nutrients.

"If you don't suffer, you won't gain wisdom."

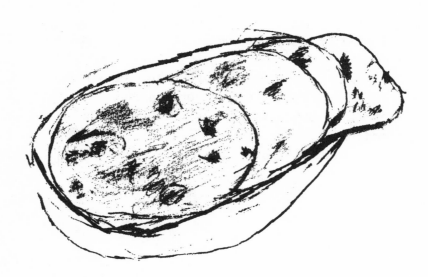

Mkate
Home-made Bread Rolls

1 package dry yeast
1/4 cup hot water
1 egg
3 teaspoon sugar
3/4 cup hot water
1 tablespoon oil
1 teaspoon salt
2-1/2 cups all purpose flour

1. In a large bowl mix yeast with 1/4 cup water and stir until yeast dissolves.
2. Add the rest of the ingredients into the bowl (except flour) and mix well.
3. Add flour to mixture. The consistency of dough should be a little softer than pizza dough.
4. Divide dough into 8 equal parts and place on an 8 inch round oiled and floured pan.
5. Place on top of the stove and let it rise for 30 minutes.
6. Preheat oven to 350 degrees for 10 minutes before you start baking. Bake until rolls are golden brown, about 15 minutes.

Serves 8.

This recipe was shared with me 11 years ago when our family first met Nawanga Khalayi (Kathy Wilson). Nawanga came to live with us when we were expecting our younger daughter, Lutomia. I had to stay in the hospital for several weeks confined to complete bed rest before Lutomia was born. Nawanga helped take care of our three-year old daughter, Muyoka during my absence. She made these wonderful bread rolls just about every day, and always brought me a sample of her daily batch to the hospital, which meant so much to me.

She continued to bake these delicious rolls while I was recovering at home every day. Mkate literally became our staple food during that time. Nawanga lives in a different city now, but whenever we see each other, we break bread together — in the form of *Mkate*. In July 1994, Nawanga traveled with us to our homeland, Kenya. She managed to arrive in Nairobi two days before we did. When we showed up at my sister's house where she was staying, she welcomed us home with a basket full of these wonderful rolls, along with freshly brewed, fragrant Kenyan tea. After having eaten air plane food, we practically inhaled the gracious offerings. It was a grand and wonderful reunion on Kenyan soil.

"You deserve what you serve."

Sukuma Wiki
Collard Greens

2 bunches fresh collard greens
1 medium onion, chopped
1 teaspoon margarine
1/2 teaspoon curry powder
Salt to taste
1 cups shredded cabbage (optional)
1/4 cup half-and-half (optional)

1. Wash and chop collard greens.
2. Saute onion in margarine.
3. Add curry powder and salt.
4. Add collards and mix well. Then add cabbage.
5. There should be a little moisture in the collards to cook with. Add half-and-half.
6. Simmer for 5 minutes or until cooked.
7. Serve with any carbohydrate and curry dishes.
   Serves 6; more if cabbage is added.

Sukuma Wiki in Swahili means "push the week." The expression stems from the fact that it is eaten every day by most families in East Africa. For that reason the vegetable "pushes" the week in the sense of economic survival. It is a relatively inexpensive and readily available vegetable, it is cooked in many different ways. This recipe is just one of the most common ways to prepare it.

Serve with *ugali,* rice or any complex carbohydrates.

It is rich in vitamin A and calcium.

"Where there is no wealth, there is no poverty."

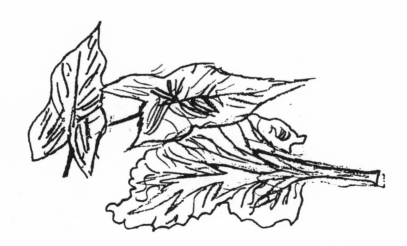

Kabichi
Cabbage

1 medium-large onion, chopped
1 teaspoon margarine
1 medium head cabbage, shredded
1 teaspoon curry powder
Salt or seasoning salt to taste
3 carrots, shredded
1/4 cup halt-and-half (optional)

1. Saute onion in margarine.
2. Add cabbage, turn for a few minutes until half cooked.
3. Add curry and salt and stir well.
4. Add carrots, stir and cook on low heat until vegetables look cooked. Do not over-cook.
5. Add half-and-half.
6. Serve with any carbohydrate and curry dish.
    Serves 6 to 8.

Cabbage is a universal vegetable and can be cooked in countless different ways. This recipe is one of many —in Africa alone. Cabbage by itself is not the most popular vegetable because of the abundant gas it contributes to the digestion process. It is also not well liked because it appears more than frequently on the tables of most boarding schools in Africa, and people who have attended those places of education may never want to see it again.

Cabbage supplies the body with fiber and vitamins.

"Fine words don't produce food."

Sukama Wiki Na Kabichi
Collard Greens and Cabbage

1/2 pound minced meat (hamburger) or ground
   chicken or turkey
1 medium onion, chopped
1/2 teaspoon curry powder
Salt or seasoned salt to taste.
1 bunch fresh collard greens, chopped
1 medium cabbage, chopped

1. In a deep pan saute meat until all extra fat has melted off the meat.
2. Drain all the fat out of meat.
3. Add onions to the meat and stir.
4. Add curry powder and salt and stir.
5. Add collard greens and stir.
6. Cook, covered for 5 minutes at medium heat. Do not burn.
7. Add cabbage and stir until cooked.
8. Serve with any carbohydrate and curry dish.
     Serves 10 or more.

This is one of the most commonly eaten combinations of vegetables in East Africa, and is served both in rural and urban areas. These vegetables are inexpensive and easy to prepare in a very short time. Meat may be added to improve the taste of this dish. This combination is generally served with *ugali* and rice, and is a good supplier of fiber and vitamin A.

"A hungry chicken wakes up early."

Okra

1/2 pound minced meat (hamburger)
1 medium onion, chopped
1/2 teaspoon fresh garlic, grated or pressed
1 teaspoon curry powder
1 package frozen okra (10 ounces) or 1 pound
fresh okra, chopped
2 large fresh tomatoes, chopped or 1 can tomato
sauce (6 ounces)
1/2 to 1 cup water

1. In a deep *sufuria* (sauce pan), saute meat until all the fat has melted off the meat.
2. Drain all the fat out of the meat.
3. Add onion, garlic and curry.
4. Add tomatoes or tomato sauce and stir.
5. Add the okra and stir well. As it starts to cook, it gets more and more slippery.
6. Add water and stir.
7. Cook for 5 to 10 minutes. When it is cooked, the consistency is runny and slippery.
8. Serve with *ugali* or rice and any curry dish.
	Serves 6.

Okra has a distinct and delicious taste. It has a slightly slimy consistency to which some people may react, while others don't seem to mind. Since there are several other wild vegetables in Kenya (*murere, murunde, endelema*, etc.) which have a similar characteristic as okra, we are used to its peculiarity. In America I have seen okra used in casseroles — apparently to disguise its less attractive characteristic.

Okra is a rich source of vitamin A, and is mainly served in urban and suburban areas, as well as in the coastal regions.

"Walk carefully, your reputation follows you."

Kunde
Cow Pea Leaves

    4 cups of kunde (cow pea leaves)
    1/2 cup water for cooking
    Salt or seasoned salt to taste
    1 small onion, chopped
    1/2 teaspoon margarine
    1/4 teaspoon curry powder
    1/4 cup half-and-half or 1/2 cup whole
       milk (optional)

1. Wash cow peas leaves thoroughly.
2. Bring water to boil in a deep sauce pan.
3. Add salt and cow pea leaves to water.
4. Cook on medium heat until tender, about 5 to 10 minutes. You may steam vegetable instead of boiling.
5. Drain any excess water if necessary.
6. Place vegetable in a separate pan.
7. Saute onion in margarine until tender, add curry and stir well.
8. Add vegetables to onions, stir and add half-and-half or milk.
9. Keep on low heat until served within a few minutes.
10. Serve with *ugali* and curry dish.
      Serves 6.

Cow pea leaves are a traditional food in many parts of Kenya. Natives of Tanzania and Uganda consume the cow pea seed itself more than its leaves. In Kenya cow peas are grown more widely among the Luhya people. Due to the increased demand, it has become a costly vegetable in urban areas. In the rural areas it is more affordable but still less available than *sukuma wiki* (collard greens). Cow pea leaves are cooked in several different ways, but this recipe is the most commonly used.

Cow pea seed is available in oriental and Spanish stores in America, but the leaves may be found in the South. You may grow the pea in your garden during the summer. I have successfully raised cow peas in Portland. You may freeze the leftovers for use at another time.

Bean leaves may be used as a substitute.

"When you take a knife from a child, give him a piece of wood instead."

Uji
Porridge

4 cups water
1 cup cornmeal flour (yellow or white) or
   millet flour
1 cup milk (optional)
Lemon to taste (if milk is not used)
Sugar to taste

1. In a deep *sufuria* (sauce pan) bring 3 cups of water to boil.
2. In a bowl, mix flour with 1 cup of cold water.
3. Add flour mixture to boiling water and stir constantly to avoid lumping. As the porridge cooks, it becomes thicker and thicker. When it starts to bubble, add lemon or milk, but not both. If lemon is used, substitute water for the cup of milk.
4. Depending on how thick you want the porridge, you may add more water or more flour/water mixture.
5. Serve with bread, tea and fruits.
6. Add desired amount of sugar to each individual serving bowl because not everybody desires the same amount of sugar.

     Serves 4.

Uji is served at breakfast in most every home in the morning, and is very simple to prepare.It is a popular food for babies, the elderly and is served to sick people who are unable to digest a heavier meal. *Uji* contains a generous supply of fluids which helps prevent dehydration in the body. It is nourishing and rich in calcium when served with milk, and can help meet the fluid intake requirements. It is mainly an energy dish. When lemon and milk are used at the same time, the milk curdles due to the acid in the citrus fruit.

"People who chatter to you will chatter about you."

Mayayi
My version of the commercial product
Egg Beater

1 dozen egg whites
1/4 cup non-fat dry powdered milk
1 tablespoon vegetable oil
2 drops yellow food color or 1/8 teaspoon turmeric

1. Separate egg whites from yolks and throw away yolks.
2. Mix all ingredients in a blender or use a manual egg beater.
3. Pour into ice cube trays and freeze.
4. When frozen, remove individual cubes from tray and store in a plastic bag in freezer.
5. Cubes can be thawed instantly in a microwave or overnight in the refrigerator for breakfast the next day.
6. Use in cooking like any regular egg.

This is not an African recipe. It was given to me by a friend of mine, Loretta Thorpe of Portland. She inspired me with recipes and ideas that refer to "cooking for the heart." People concerned about their saturated fat and cholesterol consumption levels don't have to stop eating eggs. The egg yolk is high in saturated fat (1.7 grams) and therefore high in cholesterol, but the egg white has no trace of fat at all. It has a little calcium though. Eggbeater (trade name) products available in stores are more expensive than regular eggs. When making your own version of this commercial product, prepare it in large amounts and freeze what you don't use for later.

"If you wait long enough, even an egg will walk."

Kenyan Mayayi
Scrambled Eggs - Kenya Style

6 eggs or 2 cups egg beater mixture
1/2 cup milk (if regular eggs are used)
1/2 to 1 teaspoon margarine
1 small onion, chopped
1 cup carrots, grated
1/2 cup frozen peas or French-cut beans
1/2 teaspoon curry powder
Salt or seasoning salt to taste

1. If regular eggs are used, beat eggs and milk together.
2. In a frying pan, saute onions, then add carrots and peas and seasoning.
3. Stir vegetables until about half cooked.
4. Add eggs or egg mixture and scramble .
5. Serve with bran muffins and lots of fruit.
     Serves six.

Egg dishes are eaten all over the world. This recipe is a variation of how most Kenyans and some East Africans scramble their eggs. You may vary the kinds vegetables used in this dish. This is a good way to consume your required amount of vegetables at breakfast or brunch.

Mayayi is rich in protein, vitamin A and calcium, and is ideal as a light meal when you lack time or energy for cooking. You may use this same recipe to prepare an omelet.

"The one-eyed man doesn't thank God until he sees a blind man."

Saladi Ya Matunda
Tropical Fruit Salad

1 papaya
4 seedless naval oranges
1/2 ripe fresh pineapple
2 mangoes
2 ripe bananas
2 tablespoons coconut flakes (optional)

1. Using a sharp knife, peel all fruits, except 1 orange, and cut them up in small pieces into a large bowl. (Wash papaya, oranges and mangoes before peeling.)
2. Add coconut flakes and lightly mix all fruit.
3. Squeeze the remaining orange and add to fruit salad and mix lightly.
4. Cover bowl and let stand in refrigerator until time to serve.

Serves 10 or more.

In Africa we don't generally eat desserts because our meals are heavy. We eat leisurely and take our time, and by the end of the meal, we are too full (satisfied) to eat anything else. However, whenever we serve dessert, it is almost always a fruit salad. In my humble opinion, fruit salad is the most ideal dessert for just about everybody. It is good for you, it is easy to prepare, relatively inexpensive if seasonal fruits are used, and it is low in calories and offers a full value of nutrients.

Fruit can be the dessert at every meal. I simply vary the fruits, and select ripe pieces when they are at their best.

Many of the desserts from the Western culture are delicious, but they are fattening, too sweet, have minimal nutrients, and often take a lot of time and expense to prepare.

Fruit salad or just regular fruits are my all-time favorite choice for dessert. Fruits are rich in vitamin C and vitamin A.

The most common way of eating fruit in Africa is peeling it (if necessary) and eating it the way it comes. Most Africans prefer hand peeled oranges to the knife-peeling method. Hand-peeled oranges supply you with more pulp which is better for the digestive system. Instead of putting a banana in a bowl and adding ice cream to it, just peel the banana and eat it plain. Eat as many varieties of fruits as possible.

"Don't try to carry water in a basket."

Machungwa
Orange Slices

4 seedless navel oranges

1. Wash and slice oranges, or hand-peel them.
2. Serve slices in a decorative fashion or break up the wedges and serve.
3. Eat with your (washed) fingers.
      Serves four.

Oranges are a tropical fruit, and are a favorite dessert in my country whenever they are in season. Few fruits match the richness, flavor and generous amounts of juice this citrus fruit offers.

"Fruit that isn't ripe doesn't fall to the ground."

Chai
Kenyan Tea

1-1/2 cups water
Pinch of ground cardamom
A knob of fresh cut ginger
1/2 teaspoon tea leaves
Sugar to taste (optional)
2-1/2 cups whole milk or 2% milk

1. In a small deep pan, add spices to water and bring to boil.
2. Add tea leaves and immediately add the milk.
3. Cook on high heat until tea boils. Watch it closely so that it does not boil over.
4. Sieve tea into a tea pot and serve with snack or after a meal.
      Serves four.

Tea is the second largest export commodity of Kenya, (tourism is number one) and is the most popular hot beverage in East Africa — even in hot weather. There, you will often hear the cliche, "any time is tea time." This is true because any time you visit with someone, the first beverage you are offered is tea, while the meal is being prepared. Kenyan tea has a pleasant taste and flavor because of the spices used in preparing the drink, and with milk added, is nutritious and more satisfying, and becomes a good source of calcium and energy.

The additional spices may be varied as desired. I use cinnamon, cardamom, ginger, cloves and allspice. Try these and others which you may discover on your own. The tea drinking habit in East Africa is the result of British influence, and the spices were introduced to the region by early Portuguese, East Asian and Arab traders.

"If you know the beginning, the end will not trouble you."

Matunda Ya Tangausi
Ginger Drink

1 orange concentrate (12 ounces)
2 tablespoons ginger, grated
2 cups water
1 fresh lemon or lime
2 tablespoons sugar

1. Make orange juice following directions on the can.
2. In a blender, blend grated ginger, squeezed lemon/lime, water and sugar.
3. Using a large sieve, strain mixture and add to orange juice.
4. You may add more sugar if desired.
5. Let stand in refrigerator for at least 1/2 half hour before serving to let the ginger flavor blend into the juice.
6. Serve with any meal or snack.
Serves 10 or more.

This recipe was shared with me by a friend from West Africa where the ginger is first boiled and then brewed overnight before it is used in the drink. This process takes out some of the fresh natural herbal qualities of the root. For that reason I prefer to use fresh ginger.

This is an exotic, delicious drink when properly prepared.

"Eat a little, save a little, don't forget tomorrow."

The Hungry Child Of Africa

The African child knows all about pain and hunger,
The misery of starving is for the weak and the younger.
Flies crawl around eyes that are tear-filled and sore,
And the world spins by without doing anything more.

The mother who cradles her crying child,
Looks down on the infant, crazed and wild.
With a heart that is breaking she knows her child's fate,
If only she could stop the rivers of hate.

In a world of abundance, a harvest of gifts,
Her child is dying, his head he can't lift.
Hopeless and helpless she stands silently by,
While her heart's blood takes his last breath and last sigh.

Grace Kuto

East African Diet History

In the many works on African cooking, little has been said about the healthy and nutritional values of the traditional African diet. The pre-colonial diet was based on milk, legumes, fruits, vegetables and grains. Among most tribes in East Africa (except for nomads) meat is consumed less frequently in comparison to the western world. (In coastal and lake areas, fishing rather than hunting provides the animal protein).

Due to their mobile lifestyle, the nomadic tribes in East Africa consume a great amount of meat—which has a high cholesterol content—yet they show the least levels of cholesterol in their blood. Commonly mentioned in early

European accounts, the African diet in general consisted solely of sesame seeds *(sim sim),* rice, corn, millet, beans, peas, squash, pumpkins, yams, sweet potatoes, okra, nuts, collard greens, mushrooms, berries, mangoes, etc., which made for an ideal diet. The production of food in East Africa is mainly hampered by drought, floods and conflict.

In the case of the meat-eating nomads, it was proven that the frequency and length of time spent on physical activity is more important than the amount of fat one consumes. One study by cardiologist M. John Murray of the University of Minnesota, examined the specific components of the Masai diet. The study revealed that 70 percent of the Masai diet consists of animal fat (milk, blood and meat) yet their active lifestyle was the contributing factor to their robust health.

In traditional African cooking salt or sugar are rarely added in the process. Salt and sugar were introduced in the African diet by early travelers and explorers from Arabia, East Asia, Portugal and several European countries — Britain, Germany and France. Other spices appeared in the late 19th and early 20th centuries and were incorporated into dishes.

What is perceived as African cooking today, especially in urban and suburban areas, has been influenced by Arabian, Indian and European flavors and ingredients. During the pre-colonial period, studies showed that hypertension, high blood pressure — a condition associated with excessive salt intake leading to heart attacks and strokes — was almost non-existent among native Africans.

Diabetes was just as rare in pre-colonial times. With the adoption of the western diet and habits, including smoking and and the excessive use of alcoholic beverages, diet-related diseases are more common and are more prevalent in urban and suburban areas.

According to studies presented at the Fourth International Conference on Hypertension in Blacks (ICHB) in Nairobi, Kenya in 1989, the rate of hypertension is eight times greater in Nairobi than in the rural parts of Kenya. One particular study conducted by Kenyan medical experts disclosed that the incidence of hypertension among the Masai and Samburu tribes is almost non-existent. Those ethnic groups which have maintained their traditional lifestyles and diets have managed to escape the dilemma of serious health problems.

During the conference it came to light that hypertension has reached epidemic levels among black people all over the world. In the United States black hypertensives suffer two to three times the rate of strokes, twice the rate of heart failure and up to eighteen times the rate of kidney disease as white hypertensives. Based on these trends, some medical experts conclude that black people may have a hereditary trait that is more sensitive to sodium, smoking and excessive alcohol intake. Black people may need to choose their foods more carefully and avoid the harmful elements in their diet and lifestyle.

Balanced Nutrition

Eating "right"—choosing food for good health—is made easy when we understand simple nutritional facts.

Nutrition is the science of body nourishment and deals with food nutrients, their characteristics, sources and functions. This science reveals the facts of what happens when inadequate or excessive amounts of nutrients are consumed by the body and discusses the interaction of nutrients in the body.

There are six classes of nutrients the body requires in order to maintain balance and health:

1. Carbohydrates.
2. Protein.

3. Fat.
4. Vitamins.
5. Minerals.
6. Water.

These nutrients are discussed individually here as they relate to the East African diet. Each nutrient has its own particular function yet several nutrients must combine in order to best benefit the body. A balanced diet is achieved by consuming a wide variety of foods containing different nutrients and chemicals.

I encourage you to try out as many recipes as possible. If you are not familiar with the type of food in this book, you are in for a treat of experiencing new and exciting tastes which you can add to your established diet.

1. Carbohydrates

Starches (complex) and sugars (simple) are two main carbohydrates. Complex carbohydrates are the preferred form of carbohydrates for the human diet. The primary function of carbohydrates is to provide energy, which helps the body to maintain temperature and the use of other nutrients.

The major sources of carbohydrates in the East African diet are maize (corn), millet, sorghum, rice, cassava, native sweet potatoes, yams, green and ripe bananas and Irish potatoes. Complex carbohydrates are more popular than simple carbohydrates because most Africans eat the traditional foods and are vigilant about processed foods.

The recipes demonstrate that most foods are eaten in their most original form.

2. Protein

Protein is needed for growth and cell repair— it maintains and builds tissue. People under the age of 18 need more protein than older people. Protein also provides amino acids for the synthesis of all enzymes, all antibodies and certain hormones. Protein serves as a secondary source for energy. If a diet doesn't consist of adequate carbohydrates, proteins are broken down to provide energy, preventing them from performing their primary function. Protein is derived from animal and plant foods.

A typical East African diet is comprised of more plant than animal protein. Plant foods are not only more readily available but are more economical, and are healthier for consumption than animal protein. Since the protein in plant foods is incomplete, grains must be served with vegetables in order to provide complementary amino acids.

The most common plant protein sources are: beans, lentils, peas, ndengu (mung beans), groundnuts (peanuts) and sim sim (sesame) seeds. The main animal protein sources are fresh milk, maziwa lala (buttermilk), eggs, fish, poultry, beef and game meats. The Masai and Samburu tribes depend more on animal protein than plant protein due to their nomadic lifestyle.

3. Fats

Fat supplies the body with vital fatty acids which are necessary to maintain a healthy balance. Fat carries fat-soluble vitamins (A, D, E, and K), insulates the body and at the same time cushions vital organs.

There are three classifications for fat:

... Saturated fats from animal sources, as well as coconut, palm and hydrogenated oils. Saturated fats are solid or semi-solid at room temperature.

... Mono unsaturated fats include olive and peanut oil and avocado fat.

... Poly unsaturated oils include corn, sunflower and all other vegetable oils.

Cholesterol is found only in animal fats.

Most health organizations, including the Food and Drug Administration and the American Heart Association, recommend that the average daily diet not contain more than 30 percent fat. Although fat is needed, excessive fat — especially saturated — tends to raise the cholesterol buildup in the body's arteries which in turn may cause coronary heart disease.

Cholesterol comes in low-density lipoprotein (LDL) and in high-density lipoprotein (HDL). It is the latter which leads to heart disease. High blood pressure as well as high blood cholesterol are the main causes for coronary problems. Smoking is the third enemy to good health.

4. Vitamins

Most authorities on nutrition recommend that a well balanced diet contains the required daily supply of the thirteen vitamins the body requires.

However, some people—especially in western cultures—feel that taking a multivitamin daily provides additional dietary benefits, which is not necessarily true.

There are two types of vitamins, fat-soluble and water-soluble. The fat-soluble vitamins are stored in the body (A, D, E and K. Water-soluble vitamins (C and the B series) are processed by the body but not stored. Since the fat-soluble vitamins are stored in the body, toxicity can occur if excess amounts are consumed.

Vitamin A helps to build body cells, and is best known for enabling us to see in dim light, and for preventing certain eye diseases. In East Africa, vitamin A is found in milk, carrots, sweet potatoes, sukuma wiki (collard greens), kales and other local green leafy vegetables. It is easy to obtain enough of this vitamin as it comes in concentrated amounts, e.g. 1/2 cup of sweet potatoes provides you with 150 percent of the "Recommended Dietary Allowance."

Vitamin D helps in building bone tissue and absorbing calcium from the digestive tract. The Kenyan diet derives vitamin D from fish, fortified milk, and other dairy foods. Since Kenya lies on the equator, there is plenty of sunshine all year which helps convert provitamin 7-dehydrocholesterol in the skin into vitamin D.

Vitamin E protects vitamin A and unsaturated fatty acids from destruction by oxidation. The main sources for vitamin E in East Africa are vegetable oils, green leafy plants, whole grains and egg yolk.

Vitamin K acts as a blood clotting agent. The main sources of vitamin K are green leafy vegetables. The body also produces its own supply in the intestines.

Vitamin C forms the substances that literally hold the cells and the body together. It is instrumental in healing wounds and increases resistance to infection. Kenyan diet derives this vitamin from green leafy vegetables and the plentiful supply of tropical fruits (see glossary) provides Vitamin C for the Kenyan diet. Several species of wild fruits are disappearing due to the harvesting of forests caused by the demands of a growing population for firewood.

Vitamin B series:

B (niacin) promotes healthy skin and nerves, aids the digestive system and keeps up our energy level. Natural sources of this vitamin in East Africa are beef, fish, poultry and ground nuts (peanuts). Large doses of niacin lower levels of LDL cholesterol and triglyceride while raising levels of HDL cholesterol.

B_1 (thiamin) contributes to the functioning of the ner-

vous system, enhances normal appetite and assists in sup-
plying energy to the body. This nutrient is needed in small
amounts. In East Africa it is found in ground nuts (peanuts)
and cashew nuts.

B_2 (riboflavin) promotes healthy skin and eyes, and
also helps in the utilization of energy. Fresh fruits and maziwa lala (buttermilk, sour milk) are excellent sources of this
nutrient in Kenya.

B_6 assists in the regeneration of red blood cells and
regulates the use of protein, fat and carbohydrates. This vitamin is mainly found in bananas, millet and meats in the
Kenyan diet.

B_{12} helps to maintain nerve tissue and blood forma-
tion. This nutrient is only available in animal foods. It is
important for vegetarians to take vitamin B12 supplements.
In Kenya, B 12 is found in beef, fish, poultry, eggs and other
dairy products.

5. Minerals

Minerals are necessary for body building and regulatory functions. Six primary minerals are recommended for
daily requirements and include calcium, iron, phosphorus,
iodine, magnesium and zinc. Smaller amounts of nine other
minerals make up the daily requirement. For the sake of
brevity, only calcium and iron are discussed in detail.

Calcium is responsible for maintaining healthy bones
and regulatory functions in the blood serum. The best
source of calcium is milk—in East Africa fresh milk is
mainly served to children. In several tribes, some adults prefer it to buttermilk. Milk is one of the main foods in the high
protein diet of the Masai people. Other sources of calcium
in East Africa are varieties of wild green leafy vegetables,
sukuma wiki (collard greens), kale, etc.

Iron combines with protein to form hemoglobin (red substance in the red blood cell) and transports oxygen to all parts of the body. Menstruating and pregnant women require larger amounts of iron in their diet during those periods. (Due to the lack of iron in their diet many expecting mothers are anemic in East Africa.)

Sources of iron include animal liver and other meats which are consumed less frequently. Although legumes are a steady diet, they don't contain large quantities of iron. The type of iron found in vegetable foods is not as easily absorbed in the body in comparison to the iron originating from animal foods.

6. Water

Next to air, water is the most necessary substance for life support. Most people do not think of water as a nutrient, yet it is one of the most important ones. We can go without food for months or more, but without water, we can only survive a few days. Water accounts for about 60 to 70 percent of our body weight.

Water is a major component of our body tissue and acts as a solvent, regulates body temperature, carries nutrients and oxygen to the cells and washes wastes and toxigens out of our bodies by way of perspiration, tears and urination. Low water intake has been linked to an increased risk of kidney stones in people.

Eight to ten eight ounce glasses are considered the ideal amount of daily water consumption—elderly people, breast-feeding mothers and athletes need more water than the prescribed eight glasses. Ideally, this quantity is in addition to other beverages and is not a substitute. Water is the most ideal thirst quencher since it has neither calories nor harmful chemicals.

Limit the intake of other beverages because some of their contents are not necessarily healthy. Alcohol is a toxic substance; coffee stimulates adrenal glands, while some processed fruit juices contain a lot of sugar and stimulate the pancreas. Soda pop contains sodium and raises body acid. A 12-ounce soda has an equivalent to eight teaspoons of sugar. These drinks tax the body more than cleanse it.

Due to East Africa's tropical climate people drink more water to quench their thirst than any other liquids. (Commercial beverages are expensive.) Drinking the daily required amount of water calls for discipline. For those struggling with that issue, here are some tips to make it easier for you:

1. Use a large plastic container with lid and straw (at least 32 fluid ounces). Fill it with water every morning and let it be your companion for the day. Sip on it frequently, refill it. You may flavor your water with fresh lemon juice or even milk.

2. Just before you go to bed, drink a medium-large glass of water every night. If you drink 64 fluid ounces during the day and 12 fluid ounces at bedtime, you will have supplied your body with the right amount of water.

3. If that method is impractical for your lifestyle, just drink as much water as you can with every meal including breakfast. Consume at least two ten-fluid ounce glasses per meal.

Remember the human body responds according to Pavlov's theory. Start conditioning your body by drinking more water and your body will soon demand it. Try it. You will be amazed how quickly your habits change.

Fiber, though not necessarily a nutrient, is an important part of our diet. Also known as roughage, it is the (rough) material found mostly in fruits, vegetables and whole cereals. Cellulose, a component of dietary fiber helps with digestion and elimination. Some research evidence suggests that the adequate consumption of fiber plays a role in the prevention of some types of gastro-intestinal cancers.

The traditional East African diet is especially rich in dietary fiber which is found in fruits, vegetables and whole grains. Most of these foods are eaten frequently and in their natural form. My favorite comment about the African diet is that we eat our foods the way they were created.

Legumes are of important nutritional value to the African diet. Legumes are comprised of beans, peas, and lentils, and are the main source of protein in the diet of most African rural communities. These beans are low in fat, inexpensive and can be prepared in many different ways. Some of your favorite recipes in this book may turn out to be the legume dishes. Beans come in all shapes and sizes and are readily available. The most common varieties in East Africa are kidney beans, black beans, mung beans *(ndengu),* navy beans, cow peas (black-eyed beans), pinto and red beans.

For years in the western world, beans had the reputation of being the "poor man's meat." However, with recent discoveries on the bean's nutritional value, their reputation is slowly improving, and a good selection of recipes for bean dishes is available. I hope that you try the bean recipes in this book and begin including them in your diet.

All beans except soybeans do not solely consist of protein, which can be easily overcome by serving them with rice or other grains, nuts or a small amount of chicken or lean beef which help to flavor the beans. These meat additions complete the amount of protein in legumes by providing complementary amino acids. Beans are also a good source of iron. A cup of most (cooked) legumes supplies about 25 percent of the RDA of iron for women and 40 percent for men. The iron found in legumes however is non-hemo iron which the body doesn't absorb as well as the hemo iron found in animal foods. By consuming foods rich in vitamin C, you can increase the absorption of the non-hemo iron.

Legumes are an excellent provider of fiber in the African diet. They contain about nine grams of fiber per cup— both soluble and insoluble. Soluble fiber helps lower cholesterol levels and controls blood sugar. The insoluble fiber increases stool bulk, minimizes occurrences of some digestive disorders and may help prevent colon cancer. Black, navy and kidney beans are among the highest in fiber and provide the body with calcium. They are not only a good nutritional choice but are economical, keep well, are easy to cook, and have no waste. It's a good idea to keep a variety of beans in your pantry.

It is true that some people are affected by the gas caused by the sugars in the beans. However, not everyone is a victim of this sometimes exaggerated problem. To prevent gas:

(1) After soaking the beans discard the water and boil them in fresh water.

(2) Beans should not be served with other gas-producing foods such as cabbage.

(4) Consume beans earlier in the day rather than at dinner time.

Groundnuts (peanuts) are the most familiar nuts to Americans but they are not a true nut. According to the Wellness Encyclopedia of Food and Nutrition, they are classified as legumes. The name groundnut comes from the way peanuts grow — the peanut pods develop below the ground. The shell and kernel are quite soft before they are dried. The most cultivated peanut in East Africa is the Valencia. It is a sweet red peanut which is more flavorful than the Spanish peanut. (It is not called Valencia in East Africa.)

Groundnuts are important in the African diet because they have more protein than any other nut and their fat content falls in the moderate range. When peanuts are boiled, their fat content is even lower than the oil-roasted ones according to the American Heart Association. Peanuts are a good source of thiamin, niacin and folacin, provide a significant amount of iron and magnesium and are rich in dietary fiber. Dry-roasted peanuts are fat free.

My favorite bean recipe, githeri , is made with peanuts. You will find it in the "Beans" section of the recipes.

In the United States peanuts are mostly eaten dried and oil-roasted as a snack, in candies or made into peanut butter, all of which contain fat. In Africa peanuts are eaten like other legumes. They are part of a main dish in boiled form, pressed for oil or ground into a high-protein flour. We make our own peanut paste (peanut butter) to use in peanut sauces. Delicious!

When peanuts and beans make up a portion of the meal, they provide the complete protein which has all nine amino acids.

Recommended Reading

African Cooking - Laurence van der Post; Time, Life Books, 1970.

The Africa News Cookbook: African Cooking for Western Kitchens; Tami Huttman & African News Services, Inc., Viking Books, 1985.

A West Africa Cookbook - Ellen Gibson Wilson, M. Evans & Company, Inc., 1971.

Cooking the African Way - Constance Nabwire & Bertha Vining; Lerner Publications Company, 1988.

Kwanzaa: An African-American Celebration of Culture & Cooking, Eric V. Capage; William Morrow & Co. Inc., 1991.

A Safari of African Cooking, Bill Odarty; Broadside Press, 1971.

Tropical Leaf Vegetables in Human Nutrition - H.A.R.C. Domen & G.H.J. Grubben; Amsterdam & Curacao; Royal Tropical Institute & Orphan Publishing Co. 1977.

Principles of Nutrition - Eva D. Wilson, Katherine H. Fisher, Pilar A. Garcia; John Wiley & Sons, 1979.

The Wellness Encyclopedia of Food Nutrition - Sheldon Margen, M.D.; Random House, 1992.

The Land and People of Kenya - Michael Maren; Lippincott Junior Books, 1989.

Glossary

Cereal /Breads:	cornmeal mash *(ugali)*, cornmeal & millet, porridge, *mandazi, chapati,* rice.
Meats:	Beef, mutton, lamb, chicken, fish, rabbit
Carbohydrates	Sweet and Irish potatoes, green bananas, plantains, *cassara* (yucca).
Dried Beans and Peas:	Red beans, mung beans, cowpeas, pinto beans, kidney beans, black-eyed beans, lentils.
Fruits:	Pineapple, papaya *(pawpaw)* lemon, lime, passion fruit, mango, guava, tomato, berries.
Vegetables:	Over 30 varieties of green vegetables are eaten in East Africa alone. The more common ones and those which have known names in English are: collard greens (sukuma wiki), kale, bean leaves, cowpeas leaves, pumpkin leaves, cassava leaves, spinach, cabbage, sweet potato leaves, mustard greens, okra.
Dairy Products:	Sweet milk, buttermilk *(maziwa lala)*, cheese.

Note

To learn more about African food and cooking in Portland, Oregon, call Portland Community College - Cascade Campus for information on African cooking classes - (503)244-6111.

For catering services in the Portland area call Africa Cuisine Catering, (503) 543-3812.

To taste authentic East African food in Seattle, Washington, contact:
Kilimanjaro Restaurant - Pioneer Square,
210 S. Washington Street, - Telephone: (206) 467-9593

For catering services in the Seattle area, call
Kenyan Kitchen Catering - Telephone: (206) 248-9465.

Ideas

How you or your organization can benefit from this book's proceeds:

1. Identify your or your organization's project and purpose either in the United States or Africa.

2. Contact the author at (503) 245-3812 for details.

Following are examples of just some of the projects that could be sponsored. You may know of others.

• Educational or human development projects in Africa.

• African awareness cultural programs in America.

• Trips to Africa for humanitarian purposes or for your own cultural awareness.

• Exchange students trips to Africa.

• Social programs in the United States to develop and maintain strong family unity.

Paul, Muyoka, Lutomia and Grace Kuto

To contact **Grace Kuto** for Information on how you can help in this endeavor call 245-3812.

To order additional copies of

Harambee! African Family Circle Cookbook

Please send _____ copies at $14.95 for each book, plus $3.50 shipping and handling for the first book, $2 for each additional book.

Enclosed is my check or money order of $_____
or [ ] Visa   [ ] MasterCard
#_____ Exp. Date _____/_____
Signature _____
Phone _____

Name _____
Street Address _____
City _____
State _____ Zip _____

(Advise if recipient and mailing address are different from above.)

For credit card orders call:
800-985-7323

or

Return this order form to:

BookPartners, Inc.
P.O. Box 922
Wilsonville, Oregon 97070

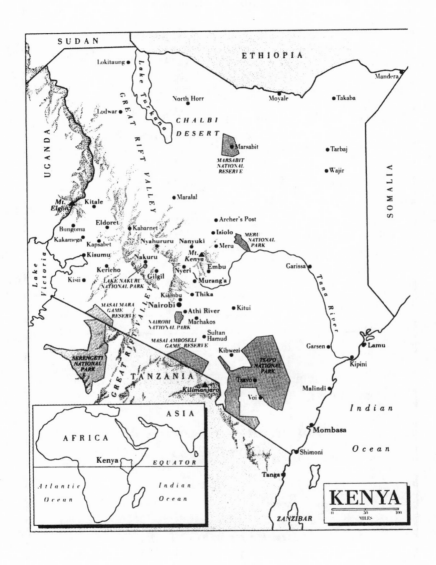